FROM VICTIM TO VIRTUOUS *for* TEENGIRLS

FROM VICTIM TO VIRTUOUS *for* TEENGIRLS

HIDDEN IN THE SHADOW OF BROKENNESS...I HURT TOO!

YOLANDA MARSHALL

Copyright © 2012 by Yolanda Marshall
Glimpse of Glory Christian Book Publishing
P.O. Box 94131
Birmingham, Al 35220

Unless otherwise noted Scriptures are taken from King James Version Bible.

All rights reserved. No part of this publication may be reproduced, stored in a retrieval system or transmitted, in any form, or by any means, electronic, mechanical, recorded, photocopied, or otherwise, without the prior permission of the copyright owner, except by a reviewer who may quote brief passages in a review.

ISBN: 978-0-983-32210-8

Printed in the United States of America

CONTENT

FROM VICTIM TO VIRTUOUS 9
   THE VIRTUOUS TEENGIRL 15
INTRODUCTION 17
PART ONE 25
   PART TWO 39
      PART THREE 59
FROM TRIALS TO TRIUMPH 69
   ONE: A ROADMAP TO VIRTUE…CRACKING THE SHELL TO BREAK THE YOKE 105
   TWO: SHAME 117
   THREE: GUILT 119
   FOUR: HURT 121
   FIVE: CRYING WHEN NO ONE IS AROUND 123
   SIX: VISUALIZING WHO YOU ARE 125
   SEVEN: YOU ARE PRETTY ENOUGH 131
   EIGHT: YOU ARE IMPORTANT 133
   NINE: YOU CAN SHINE LIKE A DIAMOND 135
   TEN: YOU DO NOT HAVE TO COMPROMISE YOUR VALUES .. 137
   ELEVEN: LEARNING HOW TO LOVE YOURSELF 139
   TWELVE: YOU CAN HAVE SELF-RESPECT 141
   THIRTEEN: YOU CAN HAVE SELF-CONTROL 145
   FOURTEEN: YOU CAN HAVE HEALTHY EMOTIONS 147
   FIFTEEN: YOU CAN HAVE A HEALTHY SELF-ESTEEM 151

SIXTEEN: YOU CAN HAVE A POSITIVE ATTITUDE 153

SEVENTEEN: IT IS OKAY TO RELEASE THE ANGER 155

EIGHTEEN: DO NOT LOOK AT YOUR PAST 157

NINETEEN: IT IS OKAY TO FORGIVE 159

TWENTY: YOU DO NOT HAVE TO FEAR 161

TWENTY ONE: YOU CAN OVERCOME ANY OBSTACLE 163

TWENTY TWO: YOU CAN LEARN TO PRAY 167

TWENTY THREE: YOU CAN EXPERIENCE WHOLENESS 171

SPECIAL THANKS

God, I ask that you continue pouring into my life what you want me to pour into the lives of others through my written work. I want to thank all those who support me in my endeavors. May God continue blessing each of you!

What is the definition of the following words? You will see these words throughout the book.

Victim — a person who is hurt by another.
Virtue — behavior showing high moral standards.
Virtuous -- pure, righteous, morally excellence.
Brokenness — separated into parts or pieces, shattered.
Wholeness — the concept that we contain all potentials -- potentials for any action, thought, or energy tone (e.g., emotion or feeling).
Conditions — the state of something.
Characteristics — the quality of a person.
Consequences — something that happens as a result of a particular action.
Worth — the value or something or someone.
Transition — a change from one thing to the next.
Simulating — to imitate
Environment — condition by which one is surrounded.

Source: Used the Merriam-Webster and other dictionary references online via Google search to define these words and other words used throughout this book.

FROM VICTIM TO VIRTUOUS

Many of you are victims of common conditions in your lives. When I think about the negative cycles many of you have repeated at such a young age, I clearly understand the true essence of your actions. I find myself questioning why some of you have made the decisions to move in an unhealthy direction. Those decisions have obviously moved you from maintaining an emotional, mental, social, physical, and spiritual balance. You may be a victim of brokenness.

This alone is a disease that spreads beyond measure just as cancer spreads to other areas of our lives and further damages us. This has caused some of you to become victims of alcohol, drugs, low-self-esteem, selfishness, jealousy, anger, compulsion…multi-faceted abuses from others and yourselves, and the list goes on. I was once a victim of brokenness, which adversely affected other areas of my life— but God, delivered me!

It is my desire that upon reading *From Victim to Virtuous for Teen Girls*, you will claim and receive the position God has intended for you to become—A Virtuous Teen Girl. As your desire for wholeness propels you toward a healthier and happier you, it is then that you will discover a special strength to embrace this season in which you now find yourself full with hope, faith, and confidence.

There is a gap that exists between living life as a victim and one of virtue—and it is within this void that discovery, recovery, healing, deliverance, and freedom bridges the gap between victim and virtuous. Believe me! This is a good place to be in your life, so embrace the moment and receive the truth.

The following process is needed for you to close the gap and lead to new experiences with you at the helm as a victor:

1) Discovery: You can actually identify the root cause of your brokenness and where it stems from in this process of your life. To work toward solving any problem, you must first recognize that a "problem" exists. After locating this problem you can then advance to the next level. I used the three-fold confession method, which moved me toward wholeness. First, you must be honest with yourself [recognize there is a problem]. Secondly, you must be honest with God [tell Him about all of your problems]. Lastly, you must be honest with others [many can tell you have a problem before you ever mention it to them anyway].

It is this disease [brokenness] that has caused a growth block in many women's (and girls) lives—the overall growth necessary [in order] to fulfill your ultimate purpose. Seemingly when you find yourself repeating negative cycles over and over again, the adverse circumstances should compel you to self-examine every part of your life. By doing so, you may find that what has happened in your life has had an impact on your thought processes, which play a major part in your continuing to repeat these negative cycles, even as a young girl. In speaking with several women and even studying women through observation and conversation, I have learned that a lot of issues they have today stem from their childhood.

2) Recovery: You will be able to reclaim your true identity in this process of your life—the identity that God gave you even before you entered your mother's womb. In Jeremiah 1:5 we read, "Before I formed thee in the belly I knew thee; and before thou camest forth out of the womb I sanctified thee, and I ordained thee a prophet unto the nations." A Virtuous Teen Girl! In order to move forward, you must be restored. Restoration is a pivotal point in your growth. This is a time that needs to be celebrated with self-love and pampering, and above all, you must practice "patience." You must love yourselves enough to

realize the importance of recovery and be patient enough with yourselves to ensure full recovery and put an end to the choice to continue being a victim of brokenness. Many have claimed other statuses because of our brokenness. This is contrary to whom God says you are — statuses the world has given you. In reclaiming your identity, you should partner with God to seek His help in sustaining you, even at times when you do not think you are worthy.

3) Healing: Your wounds of brokenness are sealed in this process of your life. Now that you have discovered the root cause of this disease called brokenness, and you have used the three-fold confession method, and you are now in recovery. You can get ready to receive your total healing — Now. You can expect to be healed from repeating these negatives cycles, namely bad relationships. This is seemingly the most common cycle many women (and girls) have repeated, and it is this kind of cycle that breaks us even further.

4) Deliverance: You can really experience the mighty hand of God move on your behalf in this process of your life. You are on the road of deliverance. After partnering with Him, you can expect the power, along with constant

prayer, faith, and action to break the shackles of brokenness. God wants to deliver you *NOW*. Once you are delivered, do not expect to return to where you were delivered. You are no longer affected, no matter who says you are—you are set free!

5) Freedom: You can make better sense of who you really are, without the hindrances of being a broken person in this process of your life. You are released and you are whole. You can now live the healthy and happy life you have desire, and fulfill your destiny. You must remember that you were born with a purpose. There is nothing greater than experiencing a life of freedom to build a solid relationship with God, and to be a blessing to others. He can take you to places you have never been before…He can expand your mind. He can also increase your territory.

FROM VICTIM TO VIRTUOUS FOR TEENGIRLS

THE VIRTUOUS TEENGIRL…

A virtuous teen girl is vigilant. She is important, righteous, truthful, understanding, obedient, and an overcomer. She is talented, extraordinary, energetic, nice, good, influential, royal, and likable.

Yolanda Marshall

I want each of you to understand that you will grow into a virtuous woman of God. Look at what the Word of God says about a virtuous woman:

THE Word of God says: "Who can find a virtuous woman for her price is far above rubies. The heart of her husband doth safely trust in her, so that he shall have no need of spoil. She will do him good and not evil all the days of her life. She seeketh wool, and flax, and worketh willingly with her hands. She is like the merchants ship; she bringeth her food from afar. She riseth also while it is yet night, and giveth meat to her household and a portion to her maidens. She considereth a field, and buyeth it; with the fruit of her hands. She planteth a vineyard. She girdeth her loins, with strength, and stregtheneth her arms.

She perceiveth that her merchandise is good. Her candle goeth not out by night. She layeth her hands to the spindle, and her hands hold the distaff. She stretcheth out her hand to the poor; yea, she reacheth forth her hands to the needy, she is not afraid of the snow for her household, for all her household are clothed with scarlet. She maketh herself coverings of tapestry; her clothing is silk and purple. Her husband is known in the gates, when he sitteth among the elders of the land. She maketh fine linen and selleth it; and delivereth girdles unto the merchant. Strength and honour are her clothing; and she shall rejoice in time to come.

She openeth her mouth with wisdom; and in her tongue is the law of kindness. She looketh well to the ways of her household, and eateth not the bread of idleness. Her children arise up, and call her blessed; her husband also, and he praiseth her. Many daughters have done virtuously, but thou excellest them all. Favour is deceitful, and beauty is vain; but a woman that feareth the Lord, she shall be praised. Give her of the fruit of her hands; and let her own works praise her in the gates."

Proverbs 31:10-31

INTRODUCTION

ONE of the most blessed gifts of all is that you as a girl claim a young LADY's status. This separates you from any other name that is given...that is to say *A VIRTUOUS TEENGIRL*. In Proverbs 22:1 we read, "A good name is rather to be chosen than great riches, and loving favour rather than silver and gold."

All girls were born with the seed of virtue. When the seed is nourished and watered daily, it allows each of you to grow into great women of valor. A teen girl of virtue positively affects everyone in her world from her household to her school, from even strangers she might come in contact with in passing.

There will be storms in life that seem to threaten the very existence as a tree of virtue. You have been chosen by your Heavenly Father to stand. With every storm comes a new challenge. The storms may have come in the form of mental, emotional, social, physical, even spiritual abuse. Many are the violations of that which lead to brokenness—for one molestation...for another the disloyalty of someone you trusted with your life...for another constant verbal abuse—nothing can destroy any of you unless you submit to the destroyer. What I mean by this is that you may be involved with someone who is very abusive, and that someone could be your boyfriend who has given you small signs to show that he is abusive.

I want to share with you that there have been many women who have made it through some of the toughest times in life, and some of the most abusive situations. And now they are whole and/or on the road to recovery toward wholeness. You can follow their lead and experience wholeness, too. As a teen girl you do not realize how strong you are. Some of most anointed, powerful, creative, successful women today were once victims in yesterday, but they are whole now. One of these women may include your mother, aunt, or another woman that you see on a regular basis.

Many of these women are now taking the center stage in ministry and other fields of endeavor. They were once hidden in the shadow of guilt, shame…brokenness. Through faith, perseverance, and discovering a definite purpose in life—scores of ladies through the ages have reclaimed their lives and proven that being an overcomer, more than a conqueror, has more to do with one's mindset than setbacks.

There are several well-known women of God who were once broken, but each of them had the desire to love themselves, and most of all they love God. As they have broken free to bless others, so will you. Oprah Winfrey, one of my favorites, and one of the most beloved television personalities of all times, moved from being a victim to virtuous. I have been deeply blessed and inspired by her story. She has blessed millions, not only through the resourcefulness of her show covering a broad range of topics—she also gives generously to the less fortunate, under privileged, through many efforts to share the simple truth that make life more livable and enjoyable.

There are many other stories of women throughout the ages that will forever be examples of the personal freedom and many successes that result from spiritual, mental, emotional, social, and spiritual growth. Love, faith, wisdom, understanding, knowledge, obedience to God and—Action! You must move toward a better you. *Please remember that faith and prayer is the foundation for change, but action is required for change.*

The Bible also makes mention of several women of virtue—Sara, Ruth, Esther, Mary, Hannah, just to name a few—and these women had faith, too! Oh, and I cannot forget my favorite, the woman at the well. This was the woman who they brought to Jesus to be stoned. Based on their thoughts and description of this woman, she was not a virtuous woman, not a lady, yet this woman was birthed into life with the seed of virtue. She was no less of a woman than those mentioned. In fact, Jesus saw the intentions of her heart. He told her to go and sin no more. But one thing for sure, those who did this were not found without sin…so what did that make them? God allowed this woman to live a free life after she met him at the well.

You too can be free to live as God intended. I knew bondage—yet I now know freedom and wholeness. It was faith that brought me; experiences that taught me; wisdom that guided me; the Spirit of God who protects me; meekness that grounds me.

I have always believed that a person could be delivered. I didn't know when, but I did know why. Why? Because freedom and virtue is God's will. I now thank Him for what I have been through. He has given me gifts that money cannot buy. He has given me Himself, His love, His wisdom, spiritual gifts—and a deep desire for virtue.

> *"Now faith is the substance of things hoped for, the evidence of things not seen."*
>
> (Hebrews 11:1)

Now before you go on I would like to offer this prayer: *Lord, help these teen girls to love, surrender, and see themselves through your eyes — based on love not judgment. Allow them to see each other as being made in your image. Father, help them all to fear less and love more. Allow them to pray for each other's shortcomings rather than judge each other. Help them to see that the bad behavior that some of them may have experienced so young could possibly be based upon something that happened to cause them to become broken. Let them not look down on their peers because some of them have dark skin or light skin, have brown skin or white skin, tall or short, thin or overweight — they are not our looks; they are spiritual beings engaged in becoming the masters in their experiences as human beings. They are girls who are becoming more like you — virtuous. Unforgiveness, jealously, hate, envy, fear, poor self-image, and other doubts must be eliminated while they are young girls. They will not glorify any woman, man, or child — only You deserve all the glory. Amen.*

I have written this book to share with teen girls all across the globe. All of you can possess the characteristics of a virtuous teen girl and grow into virtuous women and become your best self in life. He sees where you are now, and knows your end.

My prayer is that this book will help shed light on the dark areas of your life, and help you to find yourself in light of who you can be and have been purposed to be. The path to truth and deliverance to gain freedom is for everyone. If you are broken, I am certain that this book will help guide you in a direction of becoming that whole, virtuous teen girl. So many of us virtuous women can identify with the challenges that life has presented to us, and we can encourage you. If you would be open and share how you feel with your mother, aunt, or some other positive figure in your life, you can become stronger as a child and defeat the enemy (the Devil) on every hand.

Note: My story is shared in three parts. You may have your mother (or guardian) to read each part with you to help you identify with some of the content that you may not fully understand as a teen girl. This three part story has to be shared before you proceed with the chapters in order to help you on your journey. Part two will serve as a reminder for you as you grow – not to take the direction that I took to gain love, attention and affection (feeling, liking) from the opposite sex. There are Bible Scripture references in this book that your mother (or guardian) can help you understand, too. They can also help to answer some other questions that you may have as you read each chapter. As you and your mother read my story together, I pray that you two bond even closer.

FROM VICTIM TO VIRTUOUS FOR TEENGIRLS

PART ONE

MY journey in essence does not start with me. My journey starts with my mother who realized that she was the product of a journey before she was my mother. I always knew there was something special about my mother. Well, actually, there are 12 others who also call her mother. She was definitely being fruitful. My mother would be the first to rise in the morning and the last to lie down at night. She was prayerful, generous and sensitive. She truly had the gift of virtue. She was a virtuous woman, BUT…

I can never do justice to my mother's virtue—well, the dynamics of my mother's virtue—without mentioning my dad. Her husband! Yes, he was! He died in 1997, but my memory of him is long lasting. He was tall and handsome, with those gray eyes. A good man he was, yet he was also abusive, fussy, angry…and most of all he was controlling. He was full of energy and laughter. I loved my dad! He loved his children, too. But he had a strange way of showing his love. He was a provider, yet we were living in poverty. We will take a deeper look at this later.

I now realize my mother was a symbol of virtue, but she was broken. She was very strong, yet weakened by brokenness. This was the foundation by which life began to build the person that I am today. To understand who I am today, we have to open the Pandora's Box of the journey called: *My Life.*

When I was a little girl, I would get on my knees every night and pray, *"Thou lay me down to sleep; I pray to the Lord my soul to keep, if I should die before I wake, I pray to the Lord my soul to take."* As a child, I took that prayer very seriously because I really did not think I was going to wake up after having those bad dreams of my mother being beaten by my father, and those giant rats crawling in our bedroom. I could barely go to sleep—all I heard was his loud voice calling my mother everything, but a child of God—you…you…you. I could not tell which one was worse—his loud voice or the rats squeaking throughout the night. My father even called us, the children, bad names, too.

Every morning I was awakened by the smell of my mother's good ole southern breakfast. Biscuits, eggs, and bacon were my favorite breakfast food items. When I opened my eyes, the first things I saw were feet…right by my mouth—the feet of one of my sisters. There were three of us to one bed. The bedroom was small. Two beds could barely fit in the room. We had one dresser for our clothing, which obviously was not enough space for the tees, panties and socks of six little girls (and two more to come later). Everything that could not fit in the drawers was stored in garbage bags and placed in the closet.

We had to rise very early each morning because there was only one bathroom for the girls and boys. We had to make it quick when it was our turn because there were so many of us. While exiting the bathroom, I could hear the voice of my sister, "Landa, what are you going to wear today?" I answered, "I don't know." Then, I would go through the bags and pull out something that had already been worn by one of my sisters the day before.

After everyone got dressed, prayed over our food, and ate, we would yell, "See you later, Mom and Dad! We'll see y'all this evening!" Out the door we went. As we were on our way to school, I could not help but think about what my mom had told us about our behavior and making good grades. She was serious about each of her children earning an education. She did not play about slacking in our school work. We all knew you better not bring a bad grade home or that was your butt!

My mother made sure we did our homework when we arrived home each evening. Oftentimes she would pop up at the school. You had to be on your best behavior all the time because you did not know when she would show up unannounced. Coupled with the high expectations of our making "high marks" on our schoolwork was equally as high an expectation to be on our best behavior. Good grades and bad behavior were not tolerated. Even with all of her encouragement, some of us still slacked in making good grades, and being on our best behavior. But I could not just think about my mom's expectations of our making good grades. In addition, I thought about the humiliation that I was about to face from classmates that recognized I was wearing the same outfit my sister wore the day before. You know, it was typical for the sisters to wear each other's clothes.

Oh, do not mention other things they decided to find wrong with me…my hair, my shoes, my looks…so it was rather hard to focus on making good grades when I really did not want to be there. I knew that I was going to face this issue everyday until something changed.

And looking through a child's eye, I did not see our situation getting any better. Poverty (poor, not having much) seemed to have overtaken us, and not only poverty. Unfortunately, I did not see my mother or father getting dressed for work each morning. "How are things going to get better?" I asked. Well, now I can see why my mom could not work a 9-to-5 job. Her full-time job was to raise her children. My father's monthly veteran's check was the only income, and it barely provided our needs.

Now wearing each other's clothes was not the only typical thing. It was also typical for me to wear a face of hurt and awe. This stemmed from the restless, unpeaceful, and unforgettable nights. Oftentimes strange things would happen between sunset and sunrise. To tell someone the truth about this situation, often means that the innocent are told something in response, which can make you feel like everything and anything, but a child of God. And you are often called a liar and made to feel that if something did happen—which they do not believe happened—it is all your fault. The innocent are often made to suffer for peace sake.

The older I became, the worse I felt. I knew that I was going to face so many familiar faces that did not quite understand the true essence of my position—how I was living—how I was violated—and how this affected me.

As stated before, my father only received a government check that was not enough to get us out of poverty. I remember my father doing handy work every now and again, a couple of times a month—maybe three or more. I heard he had his own heating business, but that was before my time. I am not certain what happened to my father's business. But my father had the strangest kind of hustle, and he involved his children. He said that he knew of a way to earn extra money. After he shared it with us, I thought his idea was really scary.

I had just started high school, and I wanted to enjoy my teenage years. The weekends were the only time I could think about having fun because mom wanted us to focus on our school work during the week. While I was thinking about having the teenage fun on the weekends, not run the streets but have that freedom to enjoy my sisters, brothers, and our close friends—my father had another plan in mind.

This was the earning "extra money" plan. He would order huge amounts of donuts for us to sell in the strangest, yet dangerous places—the liquor stores. As I looked at this picture through a child's eye, I knew something was not right. My siblings also knew something was wrong with this! If we ever asked him the question, "Why do we have to go to the liquor stores to sell donuts?" He would cuss us out completely. With that in mind, we had no option. Well, I guess we did have options. And that was choosing which liquor store we wanted to stand in front of to sell donuts. We were taught to be obedient. But this time it was very hard to submit to his rules.

We would gather around the room and talk about who would pair up for which liquor store. "Which one do you want to go to?" I asked my sister. Hurry up! The decision needs to be made quickly because you know Mom and Dad will be back in a few minutes, and he is going to be ready to load up.

Sure enough, when Dad arrived with the trunk filled with donuts, you better have been ready to load up or that was your butt. He would get out of the car and come in the house, "Are y'all ready?" He asked. Well, if we were not ready, he would just put us into pairs. One of my sisters and I were standing in the front room when he said, "I'm taking y'all to Avondale liquor store." He told the other siblings, "Your mom and I will be back to pick y'all up. There's not enough room in the car."

It only took us about 10 minutes to get to our destination. The frowns on our faces did not last long. Once we arrived, we drove to the side of the building, started unloading the donuts, and positioned ourselves on the small brick attached to the building that could barely hold us up. "Smile," "Smile," he would say as he drove off. "I'll be back to pick y'all up in a couple of hours. But if y'all finish before I get back, just call me." I felt as though my own father was using us. If you are thinking what my mom had to say about all of this, well, sometimes she also had to go with us.

I can remember the disappointing look on my sister's face. We were both unhappy. It was very embarrassing because we always saw someone we knew each time we had to go. Ironically, some of our classmates would show up with their relatives. We felt as though we were so alone. We thought to ourselves: "What can we do?" We can't run…we can't dodge…and we can't even hide.

The shame we felt when we had to dodge the children we went to school with, and those in the neighborhoods, were fresh on our minds. It was as fresh as the donuts. The only difference is the shame lasted longer than the boxes of donuts we were selling. Each Monday, I could only pray that I would not be criticized at school.

After this so-called hustle was being repeated every weekend, the question was asked to my mother this time. "Why do we have to go to the liquor stores to sell donuts?" She replied, "I have to go, too! That's your dad who's got y'all out there." We had to ask her everything in secret because my dad was so controlling.

The sad part of this hustle was lying about the church. Yes, my dad told us to lie about the church! We had to tell the customers we were selling donuts for our church. Actually, I was not a member of a church at the time, but some of my siblings were. The question was asked, "Why lie about the church?" He said, "They would not know. Most of those customers may not ask anyway. Their minds are on drinking that whiskey." Well, sure enough, one Sunday morning my sister's pastor announced that someone had been standing in front of liquor stores lying about the church. Oh, what an embarrassment it was—somebody must have told!

Yeah, speaking of my dad's response to the customer's having their minds on drinking that whiskey…One day, my sister and I were standing in front of the liquor store, and we approached an angry male customer and asked, "Hi, Mr. Would you like to buy a box of donuts or give a donation to our church?" He said, "No. I don't want to buy any (blank) donuts." Well, he was full of whiskey and he was going to buy more. I wish you could have seen the look on his face when my sister asked him if he wanted to buy some donuts. He just started attacking her. I was so scared. I did not know what to do. I was only 14 years old. My sister started crying and I panicked.

She told me to run across the street to the store to call my dad. I wanted so badly for her to go with me, but she did not want to leave the donuts in front of the store. I called my dad to tell him what happened. He was so angry with us. He said, "I just dropped y'all (blank) off." I said, "But this man is attacking her." Sadly, he did not arrive until much later when it was close for the store to close.

The seeds of frustration, agitation, confusion, anger

and resentment were planted within me. Some of my siblings also felt this way. After seeing the physical and mental abuse of my mother and siblings, it was hard for me to receive my father. Although I still loved him, I was so ready to move from under his roof. When I started my junior year in high school, I started counting down the days that remained under this roof. This was also the year I turned 16 years old, so I was permitted to date.

I realize that when a woman's life is controlled by anyone other than God and she does not clearly know who she is, chances are she will go through life with a distorted view of love and a false sense of who she is, and it has a way of tainting any hopes of being free to become all she can be. My mother is beautiful, and she is a woman of virtue, as so many women are today. My mother has often found herself succumbing to the fierce waters of influence from a controlling man.

When anyone yields to the influence of another, whether it is negative or positive, and they are your leader, it has a way of trickling down to the innocent minds of those who are watching — the followers. In this case, I am talking about the children. When a child sees her mother or father being influenced by the control of anyone, they will grow accustomed to this behavior that can spill over into their relationships when they become adults. They will find themselves being influenced by their peers as children. This can play a major role in them letting others think for them. When this happens, they are being taught to be followers, not leaders.

What I went through as a child definitely had an impact on my adulthood, as much as my childhood. I had developed the following mentality. I was confused and broken. My brokenness led to many dysfunctional relationships until I was made whole. When I was a child I had observed my parent's behavior, which I thought was good behavior. Much of what I thought was good behavior is what had me blind and confused for so long.

Just imagine how something can look good on the outside, but it is really bad on the inside. In this case, I am talking about people and how they behave. When we execute bad or good behavior, it often stems from what is on the inside of us. Mind you, what is on the inside of you will come out sooner or later. Ask yourself, "Why do I act a certain way? Is it as a result of what is on the inside of me?" I found myself questioning my parent's behavior. *Why was there so much chaos and confusion in the home? Why was my father so angry and bitter? Why did he use so many disparaging words toward his family? Why did my mother accept so much abuse?* I had my reasons for questioning their behavior because I was affected by it. After long prayers and constant meditation, I was afforded the truth. The truth of where my brokenness stemmed from. I hope you are not confused. Let me give you an example of where I am trying to take you.

Say you have an apple and an orange, and they both look good on the outside, but they are rotten on the inside. You do not really find out they are rotten until you take a bite. Here is the thing, before you take a bite; you kind of have that feeling that something is wrong with both pieces of fruit because you have had them for quite some time in your fruit tray inside of your refrigerator. Since you have taken a bite out of them, you find out what you were really feeling about these two pieces of fruit was true.

I had observed the marriage of two people (my mother and father) who seemed happy on the outside, but broken on the inside. In seeking truth, it was as though I had taken a bite out of an apple, and it was rotten (broken), and then an orange that was the same. When you have two pieces of fruit that you are expecting to experience a sweet, good taste from—with the greatest benefit being Vitamin C (wholeness), yet all you get is "rot," it was through this reality, coupled with observing my siblings, that God was able to gently speak to the brokenness that was within me, hold my hand, and lead me on a path of understanding, forgiveness, hope and wisdom. He also gave me the power to overcome what could have remained a setback, a permanent negative dilemma. He used it to move me from being a victim to a victor of virtue.

I thank Him for leading me to truth about where my brokenness stemmed from, by allowing me to reflect on my childhood to connect the dots and make sense out of the life that He has so preciously given me—a life full of laughter, joy, peace, purpose and destiny. To be a leader and not a follower! I am so thankful for all of His goodness. I am going to share with you some of the major events that turned my life around—toward my purpose—all by the grace of God.

FROM VICTIM TO VIRTUOUS FOR TEENGIRLS

PART TWO

WE should talk now about those dysfunctional relationships that I had submitted to and which led to decisions that resulted in me bringing two children into this world —all due to my brokenness. We should also talk about how these relationships distracted me from focusing on what God had intended for me and how they played a big part in my going down paths that seemingly hindered my spiritual, emotional, social, financial, and mental growth. One of the most important things to remember and give attention to in this matter, as stated before, is that I was 16 years old when I was told that I could talk to boys.

From my first relationship, the first guy I dated (the one who I had my firstborn child with) up to the second marriage and divorce at the age of 31, I had been in transition. I went from man to man. I went into these relationships looking through the eyes of my parents. That is to say, the only things they seemed to have been able to see and value was money and material provisions. Never mind the emotional, spiritual, mental sensitivity, and provision was all about what I have come to call the "M and M" provision, *"Money and Material."*

I found myself accepting any type of behavior simply because I was looking for just one thing in a man (M and M), and I thought it was the right thing to do. But once I submitted to such behavior, everything that was hidden on the inside of him eventually showed its face during the relationship. It is what hindered me and kept me going backwards year after year, one relationship at a time. This happened because I allowed myself to become emotionally attached each time I entered a new relationship. I was a person who struggled with low self-esteem for many years, so it was not easy to walk away each time, no matter how bad the relationship was.

I was 17 years young, confused, and broken when I had my first child. I did not know anything about mothering a child because I was still a child myself. I was a senior in high school, trying to take care of a baby that I did not have full knowledge of how to nurture, other than change the diaper and feed her a bottle when she would cry. I also cannot forget that I did have to get up with her throughout the night. My mother and father enforced this because they said I had made my bed hard, so I had to lay in it. They would so often say this.

I was not financially able to take care of a child. The welfare system was all I knew, just like so many of the young girls and ladies I saw as I was growing up. I applied for welfare and food stamps so that I could provide for my daughter. I was amazed that I could only receive $137 per month in welfare. Clearly, this was not enough to take care of a child. Besides, I was nearly grown, and my parents could barely support me; and they certainly could not afford to feed another mouth and all of the other necessary obligations.

My child was my full responsibility. I had made an adult's decision with a child's mind. Because of this decision, my parents were forced to play the mother and father role in my absence, while I attended high school. Although I had not graduated from high school, I had the responsibilities of a mother when I came home each day from school. There was no mistake about this! I had to act the role that I created for myself as a mother. The consequences of my decision immediately came into play.

I will never forget those restless nights as a high school student having to take on this kind of adult responsibility. *Can you imagine how that could have felt?* I know that you are just a teen girl, but have you ever tried staying awake in the late hour on the weekend watching TV? I am certain that you were really tired, right? Well, I had to stay up every night to feed my baby, rock her to sleep, and then rise very early to go to school the next morning. This is my story! I don't want this to be your story. This is what happened as a result of a bad choice that I made.

I can even remember having to catch that big, yellow school bus every morning, right across from Whatley Elementary School. There were six or more of us waiting for the bus to arrive around 7:15 a.m. I stayed to myself as we stood there waiting for the bus to arrive. Each of us who waited for the bus was from different backgrounds, but we had so much in common. We were all very young, and each of us carried a child that we could not possibly take care of at such a young age. I was not perfect and I had not mastered my mothering skills, but it was apparent that the majority of the other young mothers also had no clue.

As we would load the bus, often I would think about and ask myself, *"Why are so many young girls even having babies?"* I now understand and I have some of the answers. Could it be a cycle? Did the mother have her first baby at a young age? Could it be because of peer pressure? Could it be because of what is shown on the television? Could it be because of what is heard on the radio? I will have to say "Yes!" to each of these questions. Just take a look around you.

I had many thoughts of dropping out of school because I did not have any parenting skills I needed. Although I have always had a mothering spirit (that does make a difference), yet I was new to the mothering experience. I still had to learn how to become a mother. It is fair to say that my parents and others always recognized me as a nurturer, even when I was very young. My dad would always say, "There's something special about Landa. She has a good heart."

I always wanted to help people. I was always in the kitchen helping my mother prepare meals for the entire family. I also helped take care of my younger siblings. As I look back, dedication, patience, wisdom, and unconditional mother's love is definitely what was, and still is, required to raise children. The wisdom of God has taught me how to become the mother I have been purposed to be, in spite of the fact that I had my first child at a young age.

My pregnancy was embarrassing. I knew so many girls my age, those who I walked to school with, who were focused on their education and going to college. Because of my pregnancy, I did not have a clear view of going to college. I did not realize how it could have impacted my life positively. But I am thankful for my sister, Cathy, who encouraged me to finish high school because there were only a few months remaining before graduation. Believe me! I really needed encouragement during this time in my life.

My first child was born three months before my high school graduation. I graduated in 1991. All of my hope of going to college had totally faded. I did not want to leave my baby to go to college. Although I still maintained the value of education, which my mother had instilled in me and my siblings, the decision to delay attending college was one of my circumstances. My hope and focus was to be there for my baby until she was older.

Do you remember me telling you about how I was ready to get out from under my father's roof? Well, the time had come. I was just turning 18 years old, when my child's father and I moved in together. We moved into this community which appeared to be safe, but later realized that we were surrounded by several people who had drug habits; it seemed like these people did not go to sleep.

Now moving in with a man was definitely something new for me. If there was one thing I remember always being told besides you need a provider, it was that you do not need to shack up with a man. Now those two things I had heard clearly. I had heard this advice ever since I could remember. Yet, this new place in my life offered something my parents, and most adults, repeatedly expressed: Provision. This, I will always remember. The decision for me to live with my child's father was a high-impact decision that has had an impact on my life in ways that only in recent years I have been blessed to truly understand.

This was a tough decision for me, but at that time I was just ready to move. And I thought my child's father could offer me M and M (*money and material*) as he proved to do as a young qualified provider. Yet, there was more. I did not quite know all that love was supposed to be. The kind of love that my father had shown all my life was both hurtful at times, and confusing. What I did know is that I, as well as my daughter, needed the love of a man who was not angry, verbally abusive, or would mentally drain me. However, what I failed to realize is that the hurting child on the inside of me had not yet been healed.

I experienced real love all right. As time progressed, it seems as though I was reliving my childhood experience of love as I had done under my father's roof. Now this was a different roof, but things seemed so familiar. Just as I had seen my father hustle to make a living and "provide" by having us sell donuts in front of liquor stores, placing us in harm's way, this was a new representation of a conflicting past which had placed all of my siblings in danger. Yes, it was quite dangerous. Well, with my child's father, I was forced to be involved in a different kind of hustle {drug dealing}—a different kind of danger.

The danger of this hustle came into play soon after it started. One night I found myself fighting to go to sleep as my child's father left to work the overnight shift, leaving my daughter and me alone with his cousin to carry out his hustle. As I tossed and turned, I found myself lying on my left side, and I could see his cousin entering my dark bedroom, as the reflection of the moonlight shined through my window, making it obvious for me to capture the view of a gun being held to his back by another man. Yes, he was being robbed — everything he had, to what was stored in our bedroom had been taken. Now here I am pretending to be asleep, yet shaking and praying that God will deliver me from this unsafe environment.

This incident was followed by another time when a stranger hid behind our kitchen wall waiting with his gun for the first person breathing to come home — he was in motion to rob us. The very next day, my child's father was upset I did not come home the night this occurred (I felt a deep yearning within to stay away on this night). He expressed that this man indeed tried to rob him and there was a great struggle between the two of them, both firing their guns as the stranger fled the scene.

This was the kind of hustle that required me to dodge

when necessary, find a hiding place, and sleep with one eye open. Speaking of sleeping with one eye open, it was true that I could only sleep with one eye open for at least a week because I could not open my left eye. My child's father had kicked me in my left eye with his steel-toed boots that he was wearing on the night of this fighting match.

This happened shortly after we split up. I guess that was better than having my brains blown out with a nine-millimeter Glock (a gun) that he held between my eyes threatening to kill me, then himself. He was doing this because I had found interest in somebody else who I thought could love me better, trying to escape all this madness of the sleepless nights, uninvited strangers—the robbers, addictive customers...it was not the best way to escape, nonetheless, it was time.

Let me say this—facing a gun was not anything new for me. The first person who pulled a gun on me was my father. He pulled a rifle on me. One day, I went over to visit my parents, only to find them in a heated argument—this was not new either. The argument stemmed from my father's decision to give one of my brothers' girlfriend money to get her hair fixed, instead of one of my sisters. I know you are probably thinking, *her brother's girlfriend?* Yes, he divided the brothers and sisters when we were children; even now the spirit of division exists within our family. My father would imply, *my sons will always carry my name, and my daughters will carry somebody else's name.* In essence, he was saying that he would take care of my brothers' girlfriends/wives before he would take care of his own daughters. This was really silly; it was stated numerous times. Now on the day this madness occurred, at least half of us were all grown up and dating. But on this particular day, the verbal abuse, which consisted of bad name calling (a female dog), was not done just in front of family anymore. It was done in the presence of one of my brothers' girlfriend.

But my mother had now gained some energy (she spoke a peace of her mind) to defend her children after many years of our family being abused, namely her daughters. Not only did my mother gain energy to defend her children, I found myself defending my mother this day by standing up for what was right. Well, as I stood up for what was right, I was wronged by having to dodge a bullet as I drove my red Nissan Sentra off the curb in fear of being shot by my father, coupled with risking being hit by a car head on because I was watching the gun instead of the street. Now I was facing two endangerments at the same time. I was not the only one in danger; one of my younger sisters was in the car with me.

What another sad image to identify with love! "Was this love?" This is the question I had been asking seemingly all my life. I was ready to experience this thing called real, love. I found out it was not in material things because my child's father gave me all of that. It was not in the money. I had a substantial amount of that, too. I had been cussed out, fussed at, had a gun pulled on me, and called bad names by my father, so I knew it could not have been in that. But the question was asked, "How can someone love you—unconditionally, if they don't love themselves?"

I had dated this "provider" for more than five years. He was definitely my high school sweetheart. After he had created an environment obviously not safe for my child and me, with all the chaos, confusion, and abuse—I knew it was time for me to move on.

So, I met a friend who I thought could love me better. Yes, this was the man I had met toward the end of my first relationship. I did not even think about recovery. We started a relationship that lasted for about a year. There I was, in transition. As we were approaching a year of dating, he formed another relationship outside of ours. *"Was that love?"* I asked myself. No, it was not love! So, that relationship ended. So many questions went through my mind. What does the world have to offer me? Can it offer me love? Can I find a man in the world who can love me? How naïve I was.

When I reached adulthood, at the age of 21, which is the age I have always considered to be that of an adult, I was introduced to what the world had to offer. Yes, I was interested! I began partying—you could not keep me out of the club. I started doing things out of my character, which was totally contrary to the way I had been raised — drinking, smoking, and simulating (to imitate) things I saw other people doing. "Was this me?" I asked. No, no, no! I was still young, confused and broken, and I had a baby. I could not possibly find love in the world.

What I did find was a man whose eyes fell upon me as I walked to my car around 3:00 a.m. as I was leaving the club dressed like I was trying to catch a man. I was wearing shorts that nearly showed my bottom, a halter-top that revealed more of my flesh, and I cannot forget those three-inch heels. After this man had approached me—with those brown eyes and standing about 6 foot 3 tall —he shared that he had noticed me in the club. I was thinking to myself: *"This might be the kind of man I need. He is handsome. He is older. He seems to be mature. You know, he might know how to treat a lady.* The question was, "Was I being a lady?"

Shortly after that night, we started to communicate. I felt the need to share with him the experiences I had in my prior relationships. He seemed to have been very concerned. He listened, although there was more. I had attracted a compulsive lying, manipulative, controlling man who only loved my body. I was silly to think he wanted anything more. Nonetheless, I found myself in another relationship. About a year later, this relationship ended. I realized he had something in common with the other men I had dated. All of them had a lack of respect for women. After this relationship came to a close, I asked myself, *"When am I going to meet the right man?"*

I will take you a little further — another relationship — another transition — and another child brought into this brokenness that was still within me. At the age of 23, I gave birth to my second child. This was a different father, but similar characteristics. This was very challenging for me because I did not want to fit in this group of having baby after baby with different fathers. I grew up in a house with 12 siblings, with the same father, so this was very hard for me. Besides, I wanted to be married with my second child, but this could not happen because I did not want to marry anyone who had the characteristics of my father.

I was young with two babies. Nonetheless, I was in transition again. I had even met the father of my second child in the club. He seemed very nice, but he represented that part of my father that was very good at describing women as female dogs. So this relationship ended after three years of often being labeled as a "female dog." I know you are probably asking yourself, "What was she thinking?" Well, the truth is, I was not thinking. I was searching in all the wrong places, looking for what only God could give. It was also nothing new to be called a "female dog." I had heard this since I was a child — so that was the "norm."

I was thankful for my second child, but I realized I chose the route of partying instead of continuing my education. Continuing my education would have closed not only the learning gaps that existed between the ages of 17 and 23 (as I later realized in pursuing my bachelor's degree), but would have helped me to focus my attention more positively. I am not saying that going to college would have prevented me from having another child, but I do believe that my focus would have been more in harmony with overall progress. By this I mean the principles instilled in me as a child concerning education would have been more likely thought upon if that choice had been made. But like most young folk, I wanted to at least try this thing they called, "partying."

After partying for years, long enough to have received my bachelor's degree, I was going nowhere and made a high-impact decision to simply shift my focus—change my life. I was partying and seeking love from those who did not know love themselves, so they could not possibly offer it. I wanted to escape the hurt by having fun, which consisted of drinking and an occasional smoke of "natural herb," all of which had taken a toll on me. Not long after this, I found myself drunk on hopes and dreams of making a better life for my family and high off all the possibilities of achieving my goals.

At this point, my heart, mind, and soul where united in truth. The truth was, I was not living life as the person and mother I was purposed to be. So, I decided to go to college, and I started in August 1998. I went full-time for years until I received my bachelor's degree in 2002. As a single mother, I knew I wanted to offer my children more than a lifestyle of partying every weekend. But one thing I struggled with was being with a man. I felt as though I needed a man. These transitions continued.

At the age of 26, I got married for the first time. I thought he was the love of my life. He was financially stable, a provider and good looking. Sounds a bit like my father, huh? You could not tell me anything. I was affectionate, intimate, and I cooked, cleaned, washed his clothes, ironed his work uniforms, delivered his lunch, took care of the children, prayed over the family, and much more. In essence, I was being my mother. That is, loving, caring, giving, and recognizing the importance of submitting to my mate. In reality, I was denied the experience of true love. I gave so much love, but I did not receive the same love in return.

Let me tell you though, I nagged, fussed, and complained. Now that was not healthy at all. I was an angry woman. I had to have the last word. In Proverbs 21:19 we read, "It's better to dwell in the wilderness, than with a contentious and angry woman." Well, that is just what he started doing—coming home late, cheating, and not spending quality time with the family.

I realized that I shared some of the characteristics of my father, too. The fussing and anger that I was used to seeing had spilled over into my relationships and marriage. I was still bruised on the inside from my childhood. The marriage had started to fade. My husband and I both contributed to the diminishing of our marriage. We both had our share of issues we had to battle and deal with. The complaining, nagging and fussing just did not go with the lack of spending quality time and cheating. Circumstances forced us to separate in

September 2001.

Six months later, I found myself opening up to another relationship—broken and confused. There I was, in transition again. Not only that, I was not even divorced yet from the existing marriage. What was important to me at that time was just having a friendship. I wanted someone to spend quality time with, but I saw someone who was very appealing to my natural eyes. He was tall and handsome. Financially stable? Well, after the experience with my husband, it just did not matter. That is what brokenness and accepting without setting godly standards will do for you.

Was he a provider? Yes, he was a provider, but not as my father and other men in my relationships had been. He, this prince charming, provided something uniquely different. He could have a decent conversation covering a broad range of subjects, laugh and joke. God seemed to be one of our favorite topics. Did I consult God about this friendship? Not right off. Did I think about my children? No. Well, that should have been the most important concern, but I was absolutely selfish. I admit that.

Can a man be in your life and not in your children's life? Yes, this is possible. Was the inner man or spirituality important to me? Yes, and since then I have come to know that conversation is one thing, faith—

practicing what we preach—is another. A person knows a tree by the fruit it bears, right? Could I have lived by myself? Yes. Would I advise women to ultimately wait on God? Yes. I have now learned that it is important to fall in love with Him in your singleness. Read on!

After a year and a half of dating this man, I was saying, "I do" for the second time. I reluctantly (to hesitate) said "I do!" I did it anyway although I was clearly warned and convinced that this was not the man for me. Okay, I was disobedient. You know sometimes you just have to learn the hard way, as my mother would say. I heard that statement so many times growing up. You may have heard your parents say the same thing as my parents said.

You see, that marriage was built on adultery—lies, deceit, and lust. Although I thought of all the wonderful things I could do to make my marriage work, I failed to realize this marriage simply would not work because it was not ordained by God. The seeds of disharmony and disobedience had been sown and I was reaping the harvest.

Prior to, and during the marriage, God dealt with me on the seeds that had been sown after separation during my first marriage. There was no peace or joy in my spirit. I began to hear sermons on adultery and being unequally yoked. Unequally yoked means that two people are not on one accord with God; so maybe the husband is saved and the wife is not, or maybe the wife is saved and the husband is not. The heated arguments in this marriage led to my having frequent migraine headaches. I was taking an excessive amount of aspirin to relieve the pain which left me with skin bruises, major hair loss, and an endoscope surgery to locate any ulcers—all due to taking aspirins extensively because of a house divided against itself.

He and I finally separated. My children and I were left living in a house with no gas, which we needed for seven months for heat to stay warm and for cooking. I was drained spiritually, emotionally, mentally, socially, financially, and physically at that point. I was broken, but I was still standing! And I am "STILL STANDING" after so many years later! I knew only God could restore me.

I was one who worried about what other people had to say. I did not want to feel the shame and guilt of my decision. We often make choices, but we fail to realize all of these choices come with a consequence. The Word of God tells us to choose life or death. Choosing life can bring forth many blessings from God. On the other hand, choosing death can bring forth many curses. (Deuteronomy 30:19). It seems as though I was choosing all the negatives when it came to my life.

In February 2004, pending a divorce, I was living a single life again, with my two children. I was still a little vulnerable, but I was committed to recovery. I was headed toward the road to healing and deliverance! I had to tell myself no more going from man to man. I had the time to self-examine and evaluate the life I was living and my actions as a result of my thinking. Living a life for God and being a good role model for my children was my first priority. A path of freedom, righteousness, peace, and truth was standing before me – and this is the course I wanted to take!

PART THREE

I was 12 years old when I first learned of Jesus and His purpose. Well, I guess I should say I was 12 years old when I gained a clearer understanding of who He is. My father would tell us that Jesus had so much power. As I started reading the Bible for myself, I learned that His power was true. Jesus was sent to earth so that He could direct us back to our Heavenly Father. I read about how He healed the broken-hearted, set the captives free, cast out devils, and performed many other miracles. He was the One who took the keys from hell.

Our family would have Bible study in our living room at least once a week, with the exception of those times my father would order my mother to wake us up at 3:00 a.m. or 4:00 a.m. to read the Bible to us. He would share many stories in the Bible of those who had been used by God before Jesus ever walked the earth. He would share the stories of Abraham, Isaac and Jacob. He told us that God is the reason we live, breathe, walk and talk. But one thing my father did in the process of us having those early morning Bible sessions was—cuss at us, while holding the Bible in his hands. I know you are saying, "You have got to be kidding, Ms. Yolanda." But, no, I am not kidding! This is real.

My father would call one of our names and ask, "What did I just read?" If we could not repeat the Scripture he had read, we were going to get a whipping. Yes, even if we were too sleepy to focus—well, that included all of us because all of us were too tired at that time of the morning. Mind you, we still had to go to school, after being awakened so early. (*I once said to myself, now how can a man that could expound on the Word of God as he did be so controlling...and cuss with the Bible in his hands?*).

Because of my father's aggressive, dominating approach in teaching us about the Bible, there was a certain fear planted within me that made it difficult for me to even want to even read the Bible. My siblings also felt the same. Since I had been an adult and blessed with a deeper understanding of the Bible, I am not only thankful God for His miracle-working power, but for the greatest power of all: The power to forgive, nurture, correct and protect. I thank Him for health and strength, and for certain gifts and talents He has placed on the inside of me and others—even for the small things that are the big things some people forget about or take for granted.

I was taught to pray every night. Even before I accepted God, I prayed. I would say to myself, "If anybody can create me, then I know they've got me." But as a child I did not know I really had to accept Him. I questioned, "Why anybody wouldn't want to accept Him?" At one point, it was hard for me to accept Him.

I got saved (accepted Jesus as my Lord and Savior) at the age of 25 and that is when I made the choice to follow Him. I still had faults, and had not yet tasted wholeness, but I learned that He had a plan and purpose for my life. I was created by Him to fulfill my destiny. I joined First Baptist Church, Acipco, under the leadership of the late Pastor Vincent Provitt. I started singing in the choir and serving God. This was a big shift for me, yet a roadmap to my ultimate purpose. I was a baby Christian, but I knew that God wanted to do something awesome in my life that was waiting to be birthed out of me in a season such as now.

Later, I joined Full Gospel Fellowship Church, under the leadership of Pastor Willie L. Brown, Jr. This church was truly geared toward helping to restore those who had been abused on some level. He definitely shared the uncompromising Word of God—he was straight to the point. You were not going to hear a watered down sermon, nor one that made you feel good. Also, he had a way of challenging his members to go to the level that God has for us all. I served as a worship leader and youth praise dance leader for a short time. I was also on the prayer warrior team and I was part of our women's ministry. This was an area of ministry that God tested and developed in me. I had the opportunity to minister to a group of women at our 2005 Annual Women's Conference. Prior to that, I was chosen to share a "Word" during the pastor's anniversary the same year, and then another opportunity prior to that. It felt good to be a part of God's family and to share his Word with others through the different church ministries I was involved in.

In the midst of all this, God had revealed to my former pastor that ministry was definitely in me. It was in 2007 when my purpose was shared through a profound thought—and that still small voice had spoken to me. The small voice shared with me that my purpose is to minister to women through my writing. I am very thankful for a new beginning and a new level!

The Bible makes more sense to me now that I have matured spiritually. I am not only looking at things through my natural eyes but also my spiritual eyes. The life of Jesus was so awesome. Yes, He performed so many miracles. Once I read the Gospels (maybe you have heard your pastor teach out of the Bible the book of Mark, Luke, John and Matthew), I learned that He spoke many parables. Even though His disciples walked with Him daily, He could only reveal things to them based on their level of maturity. It is the same way now. As I reflect on my childhood, I can see clearly that learning of Him created a desire in me to now do as Jesus did.

Just like I heard of Jesus, I would hear stories of an enemy — the kind of enemy that is common to all of us — and that is Satan. You know the one who causes the chaos and brings many adverse circumstances in our lives. Yes, he does. You may have heard of him being called the devil, an adversary and the prince of the air. Satan is just the plan old evil one.

When I was a child I would often be attacked by spirits, but I did not know why. I would question my mother and father about the many attacks that I was experiencing, being so young. Literally, there would be times that I could not even move my body. As I grew older, I would hear stories of how Satan knows your purpose before you ever thought about it, and he came to steal, kill and destroy our lives. I have learned that our life here on earth is all about purpose. It is about knowing and fulfilling our purpose whether we realize that or not. I have also learned that Satan will do whatever he can to take control of your mind and hinder you from fulfilling your ultimate purpose.

Speaking of purpose, it was my purpose that the enemy started attacking when I was young, like some of you, trying to block what God has intended. The things I said I would never subject myself to are the exact things the enemy played on—and has always played on. It seems as though he scoped me out as a child, maybe you, too. Okay, let me put it in another way. Sadly, the very things I observed as a child, which was contrary to God's purpose in and for the family, were those very things that the devil tried to use to keep me in prison in my mind.

You may ask yourself what I mean by this. Well, the things I thought would happened to me and what I feared most did happen. I found myself losing everything I had as a result of my thinking and speaking, which led to bad relationship choices, along with my overall brokenness.

I was scarred as a child. And the broken child that once lived in me for many, many years has just recently been healed through confession, meditation, prayer, seeking, faith and love. I was a child that missed some of the important things that I needed to be an effective, healthy-minded and well-balanced adult, especially concerning dating.

As I observed my parents' marriage, I thought relationships should be based on how their relationship was. I wanted to prevent having someone like my father, but I found myself attracting men who were in essence like my father. They were broken too. I have come to know that it is not uncommon to live by what you observe as a child. It is rather easy to accept the things that are unacceptable, because in your little innocent mind you think it is all right. I grew determined not to give the enemy any place in my life.

Before I end my story, I want to share with you how I was delivered me from the very thing that had me bound for a long time (transitioning from man to man). And the weakness I had been yielding to is what God used to bring deliverance — and that is a man.

One day, I met a minister, who happens to be my dear friend. I opened up the line of communication with him. He said that God gave him a vision that a woman would come into his life and that his purpose was for us to help each other to get to the next level. Shortly after having that vision, he said that he was led to the church I was a member of, and he knew at a youth ministry meeting that I was that young lady, because God had shown him. He said that it was something about the presence in the room. At first, I did not initially connect with the reasons for him coming into my life, but as time progressed, I began to see the scope of it.

After communicating with him for the first time, he was able to identify with my brokenness. He stated, "God wants to deliver you from people, and I can tell that you have been emotionally wounded." I was amazed that he knew that, even before I shared my story. That is the kind of God we serve. You see, He knows who, when, why and how to deliver you from anything or anyone that is not good for you. Again, it was not easy to accept the reasons for him coming into my life. Why? Because coming out of many transitions, this was a comfort zone. So my thoughts of him being the one for me is what was running through my mind. But God actually used him to help me to grow spiritually. I can even remember him saying, in the first stages of our friendship, "Yo, growing pains don't always feel good."

I must admit, I was still struggling with being patient—I was a "right now" woman. You see, relationship dependency was the "norm." But I needed to practice patience and wait on God to move in every part of my life, even concerning a mate.

I could feel the change that was about take place in my life. Something new was about to happen. I had become aware of all the things that had been holding me back, the mistakes I had made, and the bad relationships that I had gone through. God began to heal me from all the hurt and pain of my childhood and early adulthood. I began to read more and more truth-based books. There were many books that helped me, such as, *Why?Because You Are Anointed* written by T.D. Jakes! *8 Ways to Overcome Adversity* written by Joyce Meyer! *Seduction Exposed* written by Dr. Greenwald! *Expect the Extraordinary* written by Jerry Savella! *My Spiritual Inheritance* written by Juanita Bynum! I began thinking in the direction God was trying to take me. I can truly say all of these books and more helped me to gain the knowledge and understanding I was craving. This was really important because I knew that I needed both of them, along with wisdom to make better decisions.

I was determined not to get involved in another relationship until God was ready to unite me with "*the* man" He desires for me—for the purpose of marriage and ministry. Falling in love with God was all I needed. I began to see that it was more about my relationship with Him than anything else. Since then, I have been able to experience all of His goodness and glory. I can say that I was set free from the agony of unfruitful relationships. It was only because of His grace and mercy that I did not lose my mind. You see, I basically had my own agenda. I was a broken vessel, searching for love. I am now convinced that if I just wait on God, everything will be all right, and God will bless me in every aspect of my life.

FROM VICTIM TO VIRTUOUS FOR TEENGIRLS

FROM TRIALS TO TRIUMPH

I started graduate school on August 26, 2005, about three years after I gained my bachelor's degree in business administration. There were several challenging circumstances leading up to this point. I "believed" that God was bigger than these storms and could bring me out with commitment, determination, and unwavering Faith. I came to "know" during my journey through school, which was accentuated when my name was called, and I reached out, wearing a cap and gown, only to receive the by-product of all that God has purposed for my life.

The one thing to be understood without a doubt is that it is not about me. It is all about God reaching His people to transform areas of their lives, which He has offered through His divine promises. I am not confused about that, and I know that He is not the author of confusion. Now, confusion, from the very beginning of my decision could have prevailed as the enemy of the Heavenly Father's plan for my life, in this season of my life.

The peace I enjoyed surrounding the decision to enroll in graduate school which was centered upon positive reasons, was immediately attacked by those you would least expect with negative reasons of why I should not go back, why I did not "need" to go back, and why my decision was ill-timed. It is amazing what we can learn about others and ourselves when we share our hopes, dreams, goals, or plans. What I have learned is to remain prayerful and careful with whom I share high-impact matters with.

Imagine the excitement! I had beaten tremendous odds and overcame many obstacles to go from a teenage mother to giving birth to a second child by age 23, experienced two marriages, and despite a life of mental and emotional abuse, I still preserved and gained a bachelor's degree with a desire to climb higher. I wanted to "be all that I could be."I wanted to make a better life for me and my children. I wanted to secure the finances to offer them (and others), the much needed support I did not have. I shared all of these goals and dreams with church folk, family, and friends who smiled in my face and spoke words of support while secretly they spoke among each other against me.

Yes, I heard it all directly and indirectly from so many who said, "How is she going to go back to school with two children to raise?" to "God is not telling you to go back to school" to "Why is she going back to school?" One thing I can truly say is a friend truly sticks closer than a brother or sister, and I thank Him for my true friends who want more out of life both recognizing and encouraging me to do the same. I am thankful for those special brothers and sisters among all my siblings who truly are friends. There are many dream stealers in our lives who walk with us, yet do not walk in agreement with us. This is something my good friend, Minister Vince Collins, would repeatedly share. I finally got it! He would often ask, "Why do you think Jesus admonished go and tell no man?" Today I can answer, but before I offer this answer there is more.

God will always place in our lives great people in times of great need. On some level I had been in a place of great need whether it was recognized at the time or not, seemingly all my life. Yet, this was a time I knew without a doubt that I was in a fight without hands, with few "hands" reaching out to help in any form. When I was wrestling with the seeds of thought that had been planted in my mind concerning "God telling me to go back to school," I had the prayers and encouragement of my friend, Phyllis. I also had the full support of my longtime friends, classmates, Anita and Shundala; and my sister Tonya. However, it was that special God-infused wisdom, knowledge, and understanding of Phyllis and Vince that really pushed me forward.

I can remember the prayers, words of wisdom, and the

scriptures Phyllis shared with me. Vince, on the other hand, had a way of challenging my thoughts. I can remember much of what he shared in our many conversations. Over and over he would say, "Yo, you have always been there for those that have not been there for you. You have a heart, mind and soul to be a blessing to so many people. You've given of your time and finances to help others. You've given of your mental and emotional resources to a fault. You place seemingly so much above your own happiness. You've been blessed with wisdom, knowledge, and understanding." He asked, "Could it be that God is about to add greatly to your understanding?"

What I most remember him saying is, "God will not hinder His own agenda." Moses was called (purposed) to do a great work. God told him that He wanted him to deliver the children of Israel out of bondage, but things did not happen the way, or as soon as, Moses thought they should. Things did not happen easily. Moses did not achieve immediate success but it did not affect the outcome. He initially reached for every excuse possible. He told God that he could not do it because of his speech impediment. God answered by giving him someone to go with him, Aaron. The outcome was successful. There were lessons learned and taught during the process. The issue was process." (More information on Moses is available in the Bible in the book of Exodus).

This one thing I do know: What God says about something is all that matters! Yet, when your desire is strong and your finances are weak and absolutely necessary to get you to the next level in your purpose, responding as Moses did is easy. Now, as I sat taking the Miller Analogies Test both the bitter and sweet leading up to this point came to mind. Yes, the money came through for me, and with only one day before classes started, there I was seated in a seat of faith and trusting God. Not only did I past this test, absolutely necessary to enroll in class, I knew that I had passed certain other of life's tests as well. What Vince had been telling me all along is something that I had believed but came to "know."

"There is no problem that exists outside of our own heads. It is how we respond that matters most." This was not only a season of challenge it was a season of growth and change. Grad school, here I come!! August 25, 2006, will always be remembered as a day of victory against all odds!

The very next day I found myself at Troy University in Montgomery, Alabama, in an atmosphere of stress and strain because of a lengthy registration process. I arrived around 4:00 p.m. that evening. My first class session was scheduled for 7:00 p.m. There I was among students who voiced their opinions about registration while I fought to focus on my journey to be there and give thanks. At this time, I met a young lady that would be God's wink of approval for one of the many reasons for my being there, and a symbolic voice that silenced all of the negative comments at my announcement of going to grad school.

This young lady and I struck up conversation amid the many conversations lending to the registration pandemonium (uproar). Immediately recognized her demeanor—that look in her eyes and facial expressions did more than suggest frustration with the registration process. She began to freely share her discontentment in the matter, but I was able to discern there was more going on with her. She shared how she wanted to give up on even trying to complete the process because things were so hectic that night. Patiently, I began to respond and encourage her. The first words out of my mouth were, "You can do all things through Christ who strengthens you." I then encouraged her to read that particular verse (Philippians 4:13) whenever she felt like giving up.

I was both honored and humbled that she could open up about her frustrations. As we talked, I could feel the deeply rooted pain. She shared enough to reveal her mental and emotional brokenness. What I have learned over the years in my journey from a victim of brokenness on the road to wholeness is that mental and emotional brokenness is synonymous to the lack of spiritual wholeness. No amount of smiles, even nonchalant behavior, can cover up the truth. The spirit of God will find us out. I was found out once upon a time, and I am thankful for this. I sincerely believe that this young lady is also thankful.

Later, as we shared breakfast one Saturday morning, I learned she was dealing with troubles in her marriage. I listened to her carefully and I was blessed to share with her from a standpoint of having been an over-comer in many of the very areas she spoke about. We prayed and until this day, I am thankful to the Heavenly Father for meeting her. I learned a lot from this opportunity to minister to her. One, she admitted that she was thankful for God placing me on her path.

The thanks she gave me, was all about Him. As she thanked me for reminding her of that special message to her heart, mind, and soul found in Philippians 4:13 a couple of weeks later, God was using her to give me what He used me to give her, "You can do all things through Christ who strengthens you." I had also shared with her some of the particulars of the struggles I had faced. At that time, I simply wanted her to know that she was not alone. In some small way my hope was that she could find strength in knowing that I had multiple peace-threatening issues that I was determined to stand up against and win. She was there to minister back to me.

Only He knows how much I needed those same encouraging words, and only He knows how much I needed that $50 seed she planted in my hand one morning before class. Let me share this, when her name was called to receive the degree, I could not help but think of both our journeys from the beginning up to that very moment. She is now happy and free, doing well and gainfully employed.

Although we have not spoken since we both graduated, I continue to speak blessings on her life. There is a passage of scripture that I am reminded of when I think of her and others that I was able to minister to while in school, Truly God; the Shepherd will leave ninety-nine sheep just to save the one. (Matthew 18:12-14). I am particularly grateful that the Shepherd used me. God proved that not only was it His will for me to get in school, He helped me to take something out of the experience. That is the truth in knowing that all the negative talk surrounding my going to school can be answered in Him placing me right where He wanted me to be. What He says is all that matters.

Remember I mentioned how much I thanked God and her for coming to me weeks later to thank me for the encouraging scripture? There is a reason. Actually, there are several reasons that started just as I started school.

Shortly after I started grad school, the company I had worked for just over two years was bought out. Before the acquisition, I had enjoyed somewhat of a financial good-health status. With base pay and monthly bonuses and incentives, there was more than enough to take care of my family, bless others in need of a little help, and have money left over. That is to say, I was blessed not to live pay check to pay check. The buy-out and transition was nothing shy of financially, mentally, and emotionally draining. Spiritually, I was fighting even harder than I was leading up to getting in school. I realized something great was being done in my life, and there is sunshine on the other side. Joy comes in the morning, yet I definitely felt the reality of a long night.

First, just before the transition that robbed me of my financial stability there was the issue of car repairs that took about $1,500 out of my household and set me back. That was one of the main reasons I was setback and was short on cash to take the pre-grad school test mentioned earlier. Why not tell it all? Also I was setback by loaning a friend some money for car repairs that they committed to pay for on my good name — it never happened. I was stuck with the $400 bill and got slightly behind on rent and other obligations. The price we pay for emotions and poor choices can affect us when money is needed to take advantage of good choices requiring money. This taught me to truly wait on God and not be in denial about the signs.

Well, there was one sign that was inescapable. This was the sign that had financial struggle and unhappiness written all over it after the transition. I realize that I'm sharing all this in an almost rambling fashion. Hopefully, you are still with me. There is much more.

Okay, teen girls, one thing that resulted from this transition was a promotion to a management position. This new position paid well, very well, but I, Yolanda, was not getting paid. Of course, this was not known at the time I accepted the position. Initially, I thought the pay increase would have filled the gap with respect to the loss of the incentive pay received prior to the acquisition. But guess what? This never happened.

I was doing the work of a manager, had the responsibilities of a manager, had a promotion as a manager complete with company memos to fellow employees, but the pay of a team leader. As a matter of fact, the more I reflect on all of the congratulations received, with well wishes ringing in my ears the more furious I would become. I knew the pay was low. The stress and responsibilities were high. Nonetheless, I kept pressing on. I performed as though I was being honored for my bachelor's degree and was being paid accordingly. That is, until I could not take it anymore. You would be surprised what much prayer and a little research can do for validating that gut feeling of truth being withheld.

The deal was that I was being used for my degree and talents to cover for a manager without a degree or the experience that this position called for. In sum, I was helping to earn her paycheck. When I think about the various protocols I developed for the department and other suggestions I had made in the best interest of all involved, it still kind of rubs me the wrong way to know that these things were often discounted on the front end, and played up on the back end as the doings of management. Of course, by now you know that management did not include me. After months of unfair wages and treatment, I learned more from the employees of the company that took over. I could see that there was no one to turn to within our local office. I forwarded my concern to corporate, and they made a mess of it all.

What is really interesting is that prior to all this

madness on the job, I had a dream revealing the spiritual nature of what I would soon experience on the job. As things started to unfold I knew it was time for me to go. Most of us never consider the spirituality of the people who employ us. Truly, we need to hold this in high account. Most of my problems stemmed from a minister's wife—a church going woman who didn't seem to have church inside of her heart. Yes, this who my boss was. What is in your heart will definitely come out. It will be shown through your actions, and that is a truth.

Through all the humiliation of being told my degree did not even matter—and being used and drained mentally and emotionally—God gave me the strength to endure. I thanked Him much then and even now in looking back. Proverbs 29:2 tells of a truth that cannot be disputed, "When the righteous are in authority the people rejoice: but when the wicked beareth rule the people mourn" (KJV). There are no limits. This can apply to your job, home, church—anywhere an authoritative position is being held.

I was in total mourning, but I knew He had a plan for my life. I knew that I had to stand in faith because the wicked selfishly didn't see the harm they were doing and causing; however, it was all a blessing for me. My time was almost up, and I had to depend on Him for direction.

I had a deep feeling in my soul there was work for me to do elsewhere.

Now all of this was going on during my first semester. There was trouble on every side it seemed. My income did not permit me to drive more than 200 miles round trip to school twice a week (on the weekends) and cover hotel costs. The money was not there and this is reality. I tried hard not to drift into a complaining mode. I was in the process of being delivered from complaining. He had placed someone in my life to help in this area, but nonetheless, money was short and I did have concerns. In the midst of it all came a ray of hope each and every week.

With all this chaos, I started contemplating, meditating, and seeking God for direction. I needed Him to make it plain to me as to whether or not my time had expired in faithfully serving an employer that did not honor or respect me, along with countless others over the years. An eight-to-five job can seem like eternal torment when you are unhappy in any situation, having done all you know to do to make things better with others involved not showing any interest to commit to positive change. I did not want to make an emotional decision. This is a matter placed in His hands and left there.

Finally, I gained peace in the direction I needed to go.

The decision was followed by a dream I had one night in which all I could remember was the chapter and verse number of a scripture without the name of the book from which it was taken. What I got was 115:3. When I awoke, immediately my thoughts fell on the book of Psalm. I read all of Psalm 115. After meditating day and night on this, I had much peace in knowing it was time for me to leave this place. A few days later, I put in my two-week notice and I resigned from this position. However, I was asked to go ahead and leave after one week. I was hurt, but I was paid for those two weeks.

Initially, I told only those close to me of my decision to leave, but it was only a matter of time before the word got out. There was negativity surrounding this decision. There will be those in your life that will talk against you simply because they have vocal cords. One thing's for certain, those who are locked into looking at things with their natural eyes only and hearing things with their natural ears cannot possibly discern what is spiritually being done.

He has never forsaken me. Through some of the biggest crisis in my life, and the life of my children, He has been right there. In the good times He was there, too. I give Him thanks during the good and bad times. He is faithful. The more I realized this, the more my desire grows to please Him and become more willing and obedient in the smallest of matters. God will supply our needs and allow the supply to get scarce in order for us to recognize Him as the source of our supply. And no matter the beginning, the end is victorious. There is a process. I have learned to appreciate the process.

It was now time for the second semester to begin. I no longer had a job, and I was not sure of all the details of how I was going to make it, but certain with total faith I had to make it. With no prospects for employment and low to no money most of the time, I, as well as my decision, was becoming suspect. You might be asking, "Why on earth did you quit your job?" If this comes to mind your thoughts are not alone. Many people asked this question, but of course I can only give one answer. Regardless of what things looked like on the surface I trusted God totally. Do you remember my sharing the conversation with Minister Vince in which he ministered to me about Moses being called to do something that did not immediately go as he may have thought, and all those lessons Moses had to learn and the strength he had to gain from it all? Well, this story had Yolanda written all over it. And it is very real to me to this day.

The question of how was I going to get back and forth to school at this point were followed by more insulting questions and comments than the going-back-to-school issue did. Now, as I was transitioning to a higher level mentally, emotionally, and spiritually don't think that the enemy did not seize the opportunity to launch an all-out attack to judge, criticize, scandalize, and defame my character. And he used as many people as he could. It's almost as though people had become willing vessels for the enemy to beat up on me.

Oh, I heard it all, "You need to get another job," "You've got two children to take care of," "You're a fool," "You're going to lose your apartment," "God wouldn't have told you to quit your job to struggle," "I'm not going to help you with money because you're able to work," "You can't pay back any money if you borrow any because you don't have a job." But you know what? Phyllis, Anita, Vince, and my sister Tonya were right there with prayer, encouragement, and just speaking life into my situation. Needless to say, I pressed on.

Now one of the highlights of all this was explaining the situation to my children. Although my son was only nine years old at the time, his response was as much a blessing as those five close ministering angels that I have mentioned repeatedly. He is wise beyond his years; he would pray and encourage me, and this blessed me deeply. My daughter was supportive in her own way yet not as vocal. See, the years of transition had taken a toll on our relationship at that time, nonetheless, I believed that this new place He was taking me would bless my household. The blessing was that my children truly understood as best they could, my passion to allow Him to fully lead us. And this He has. It doesn't mean we didn't face challenges, but we also experience some positive changes in the midst of the storms.

I was holding on by faith as never before — still holding on to my joy! Still praying! Still loving! Still caring! Still encouraging! Still laying hands on the sick! Still doing spiritual warfare on behalf of others! I was not going to be defeated. I began to notice that although people were speaking more negative now than in the past I was at peace. I could feel the growth of being delivered from people more and more. The enemy thought he had me. Satan thought that if enough negative energy surrounded me that I would give up and give in. Oh no! Even when things did not look good, I moved forward with total faith.

And, oh yes, I continued to press my way back and forth to school. Well, during the third semester with three classes left and 10 semester hours, three days before midterm exams — my car was repossessed. I will never forget my son's reaction to this incident. He shouted to the top of his voice that someone was taking the car as I studied for the exam. He was very upset. I could see the concern in his eyes. He asked, "Mom, how are you going to get around?" and "How are you going to get to school?" I assured him that everything would turn out favorably. I explained that a way would be made for me to get around and back and forth to school. I told him that we would get another car. I explained that certain things happen in order to move us closer to God and to make room for what He ultimately has in store.

Since that night God has delivered on everything that I shared with my son. I was blessed to get to school, and I was blessed to get a car in February 2007. It took some time to get a car, but I got a better car than my old 2000 Mazda. God is good!

Now, I was rather upset but still managed to hold on strong. Do not think for one moment that tears were not shed that night. Oh, yes, many tears fell. For some reason it was hard to digest the reality of what my son had witnessed. Likewise, it was hard to digest his reaction to it all. I began to pray and cry out to God. Finally, I said to my Heavenly Father, "Not my will but your will be done." I realized that I had to keep myself composed. I simply could not allow myself to become an emotional wreck no matter what. I had a test to prepare for that coming Friday, two days away. I had to find the strength to stay focused.

God always has a ram in the bush. This means that He will always provide. And He did just that. He had positioned my friend, Minister Vince, to be available and a willing vessel in that season. After explaining what had happened, I can remember him saying "Yo, you know I'm there for you." He drove me to school so that I could take my midterm for my financial analysis class. He waited patiently in his car. He would be praying for me, reading, and working on business ideas. He made a commitment to help me out from that moment on. He waited patiently from 5:00 p.m. to 9:00 p.m. for my Friday class and from 8:00 a.m. to 5:00 p.m. for my Saturday class. God is better than good all the time.

I was really nervous after taking the test. A few days later, the results were in. I did not pass the midterm test, but I remained positive. I stood on faith. I kept the voice of my conscience positive. I declared within myself that I would graduate on time. I prayed. Determined to press my way through, I immediately emailed my instructor to find out the score I needed on the final exam to pass the class. He sent an email reply with the necessary score. I had a new target. There was no doubt that I would achieve that score—with God's help. It is amazing how when we focus on something of high positive value in the midst of a storm we often forget we are even in a storm. Or at least, the storm loses its grip on us.

While my thoughts, efforts, and energies were concentrated on this new objective, certain of my circumstances got worse. The heat was turned up a notch. There is no doubt that Satan's furnace was blazing, yet the Potter's oven was heated also. On one hand there appeared to be a trap growing bigger; and on the other hand He was preparing the ingredients for triumph.

A few weeks had passed. Now it was time for my final exam in my most challenging class. As I approached this date, I was so thankful that this exam was scheduled on a different date than the exam previously mentioned. Now, I was just finishing up a major research project that was assigned in groups of two to four. The score from this coupled with the exam score would tell the story. While optimistically preparing for the test, I received an eviction notice. On the week of the exam my thoughts were forced upon the idea that my children and I could be soon without a home, with no money and no place to go. About this time, I spoke with my good friend, Anita, who immediately opened her doors to my children and me. I thanked her, but I was not ready to give in so easily.

I prayed and simply focused on a positive outcome. I approached my landlord with a plea for an extension to come up with the money. I had explained my circumstances. Extension granted! I went "to work" trying to get help. I tried my family. Well, there was sensitivity from a couple of my siblings who had the heart to help but did not have the means. Yes, and this does include doors being slammed on me that were opened to others in their season of challenge. I had been there for some even during several seasons of trial. I respect that we all have our immediate families to provide for. I respect this. Over the years I have needed some help and was blessed by the kindness of many. The thing is that when you know someone has it — and would gladly give it to others in the same situation — this can be hurtful and frustrating.

Well, I tried the friends mentioned throughout this book. Seemingly everyone was being financially challenged at this time. I do not say this in sarcasm, I mean literally. Up to this season my closest friends were OK financially, but they were having challenges at this time. I received a lot of encouragement and as much help as each could offer. This still means a lot. I can remember calling Vince after we had not spoken in a couple of months when I was first coming into this season and told him I needed a certain amount of money to make ends meet. He went over and beyond. He did not question me at all. He simply asked, "Yo, when do you need it?" I answered, "As soon as possible." He had just gotten back from a business trip and was tired. I could hear it in his voice. Yet, the last thing he said before arriving about 30 minutes later was, "I'm on the way!"

My friend, Phyllis, had the heart, but no money; she was in need too. Not long before this, Anita gave me close to $100 she had intended to put in church. Unlike the majority, she recognized she could meet a need and be a blessing without feeling guilty for not giving to the church. Besides, she said "something" had told her to hold on to it. This happened in advance of my calling her. So when I asked, she gave it. This brings me to the next place I turned for help.

I cried out to God, but the answer did not come immediately. But one day on my lunch break while working a temporary job I had just been assigned to, the answer came—churches. I was excited. I gave honor and praise to Him for just the thought. I mentioned it to Vince when he came to pick me up from work. He looked at me and said in his heavy voice, "I wrote some churches on your behalf weeks ago with no responses. I even listed character references for you. I didn't tell you because I didn't want you to know anything about it nor did I want those I listed as references to know. I've just been praying and waiting." I remained optimistic. A letter was drafted. Letters were sent to a significant number of larger churches (mega-churches and first-stage mega-churches) as well as others in Birmingham and Huntsville, Alabama.

What I got was a wake-up call. It was God who sounded the alarm. I was blessed to receive a call from one church, followed by two Wal-Mart gift cards. I was thankful. Gift cards were not exactly what I had been seeking, but I was most appreciative and put it to good use.

The second response came from a church that sent a letter that I will never forget. What I most remember were the words—"your circumstances are not uncommon to man, and we will pray for you." My initial thought was, "And I am sure your response in times like this is not uncommon to man either, and I will pray for you." I was not bitter, just shocked. Nonetheless, I was sincerely blessed by both responses. I was blessed just as much by those not responding. Of course, this truth took a while to arrive at, but I eventually got there. Maybe, I should have sent them to the smaller churches. What do you think?

After a short time, Vince said, "God takes care of His own." He mentioned my good heart, desire to serve God and others, and live a life of obedience…he expressed his belief that God had something in mind. He truly believed that He was setting me up for a blessing so big that all of these challenges were needed. They were a part of something awesome, but it was all about God.

Nothing seemed to work. I attached the eviction notice, my impending car repossession notice, even the car repair receipt that was instrumental in the turn-around in finances. I was going to work every day but it seemed to be barely working. The temp job I was working was about 15 miles to 20 miles from my apartment. My apartment was about 20 miles from Vince's house. This was one way. Because he was working, I had to wait for him to pick me up after work. I was only working 25 hours to 30 hours per week at $10 an hour, but I was grateful. I was feeding my children and paying to get from point A to point B, most of the time. I knew this trouble would not last; it was just a short season.

Time had passed and it was now July. The weather was hot. The heat was on in my life and it was about to get hotter. It was July 21, 2006, the scheduled date for my management test. I entered the class after more than 40 hours of study over a two-week period. The room held just over 20 students. It was filled with negative energy — negative energy, due to such a high level of stress. I was not the only student concerned about this test. For me, however, I had to pass this test in order to graduate on time, and I had the shakiness to prove it. The negative vibes seemed to just zap the little bit of confidence that I was holding on to for dear life, and my energy.

It took two weeks to get the test results. I received the results of my management exam on the day of the final exam in my financial analysis class. The moment of truth had arrived. There was no passing grade to get excited about — I had not passed. The best part about this ordeal was the fact that I was able to take this test without the added pressure of knowing I had not passed the financial analysis class. Once more I could feel mental, emotional, and spiritual growth. In some strange way I was relieved. My thoughts were positive. Faith was truly carrying me, and my prayers worked! My management instructor gave students the opportunity to perform one more analysis. You remember my sharing that a certain test score was needed to pass? We will later see what the result was.

The financial analysis test was taken. The management class results had been revealed. A bonus project had been assigned. My thoughts were moving in so many directions. My faith was strong, yet reality struck. I was headed back to Birmingham in the car with classmate/project partner. We had worked together on several projects in management class all year. Only, she had done enough to pass the class, I, on the other hand was dealing with the reality of her absence on that "blessed" bonus project that I so desperately needed in order to "walk" in December.

The pressure was on. The financial analysis instructor informed us the scores would be posted on the school's computer blackboard at 10:00 p.m. that very evening. Based on his proven track record of promptness, I knew he would deliver. My concern was "what" would be delivered. I was a little nervous but still standing! Still praying! Still holding on to God's unchanging hand!

I chose to go to bed. I did not have access to a computer to get the grade, so I was forced to wait. This was a blessing. Sunday morning had arrived, August 6, 2006. I must admit, the night before was restless. I tossed and turned all through the night. I sent up a strong prayer before I lay down, and all night long I was crying in my sleeplessness. I needed the strengthening of worship service and fellowship, but was literally too weak and nervously sick to go to church. I simply had to get to a computer to review my grade. I waited until the library was opened, which seemed to take forever.

I was seated at the computer going through the motions of logging into the school's blackboard and it was as though I was looking through someone's eyes. And right before my eyes—or somebody else's—there, was my final grade. No suspense left—I didn't pass. I was lacking exactly seven points. Seven whole points! I did not fret. I could not fret. I just turned to my Heavenly Father in faith. I immediately connected with the spiritual significance of the number seven—the number of completion. I had a deep feeling in my soul that things were turning around. This was not evident based on what I could see with my natural eyes, but through the eyes of faith there was much evidence. You will see in a moment how I was blessed in all this. I now understand the depths of Hebrew 12:11, "Faith is the substance of things hoped for and the evidence of things not seen."

I needed only seven points, and it was proven that God was (and is) faithful. He proved that He would not leave or forsake me. The instructor had given us an optional project to do at the beginning of the course. Believe it or not, this project was worth—seven points. I said to myself, "Thank you God! I can handle this with your help!" Later, I called my instructor to inquire about the details of the project. I know he could feel the concern in my voice. He replied, "You can do the project, but it's less likely that students will receive the maximum amount of points." After his response, I briefly paused and asked God silently, "Where do I go from here?"

After a silent pause, he immediately shared that he would consider assigning another project, a report on Public Education Funding, but he would have to weigh it all out. A certain level of peace came over me instantly — that peace that is spoken about in (Philippians 4:7) — the peace that surpasses all understanding. I remember saying to myself, "Look at God work." All I needed was a little seed of hope. This hope was translated as the mercy, grace, and favor.

Phyllis, one of three prayer partners, truly a prayer warrior, prayed for hours, speaking life into this situation, praising Him in advance for His seven-point miracle. She stated: "It's done." We were in total agreement. Vince and I prayed after this. His statement was, "Yo, you know God would not have brought you this far to leave you. You're at the end now, and I'll do all I can to help you."

After a few days had passed, I spoke with my instructor, and he explained that he had gone ahead to approve the second project because he felt strongly that the first project would prove far too challenging to receive the maximum points needed — for me, the seven points were absolutely necessary.

The enemy, the adversary, Satan, the devil himself—was mad. The furnace was turned up to a couple notches from the max. That is to say, those things were heating up on a level that only He could cool. Before things would cool down some, I received the second eviction notice. By now it was mid-August. I had only three days to move. Three days. I knew staying focused was not an option. God had proven He had not given up on me. I had to prove I would under no circumstances give up on Him.

My plate was full. I was facing eviction with limited funds to move. I had a case study to do for the management class that normally required a group of two to three people. Then, there were two projects to finish for my financial analysis class. On top of all this, I was a single mother, with the sole responsibility to take care of my children. My heart was aching to spend more time with them—which had been limited due to the demands of school. Our transportation we could no longer call "ours," and as for our home, our apartment, it did not even feel the same. As I packed my things, my thoughts went from the journey in my life to this point. The bitter and sweet times in life make our life rich in so many ways. It might not always feel good or be consistent with the way we desire things to go, but He knows best. He was blessing me to learn. I was battling to earn my degree and yearning for a major change. My son, daughter, and I continued to pray. This is something we did no matter what. We have always prayed for others, even for the people who were speaking against us. This does happen, you know. But anyway, it was time to move.

On August 18, 2006, I moved in with one of my younger sisters. She kindly opened her door to the children and me. It was rather crowded and uncomfortable. The atmosphere was far different than what the three of us had grown to cherish in our former home. Yes, former. This was the new reality, so I just reminded myself, "Not my will but His will be done." Time was marching on. With no transportation, no computer, and with no help from the project partner and classmate I had worked with off and on all year, or any other classmate, three research projects were due. Once again, God had it worked out. Once again, my good friend was there.

Vince would take me to work and pick me up, until one of my co-workers moved in the same apartment complex that my sister was living in. She politely gave me a ride to work daily. He would then pick me up in the evenings. We would get to the library between 5:30 p.m. and 6:00 p.m., depending on his schedule and night of the week concerning library hours. Most nights we would be there until 9:00 p.m. when the library closed. I would get home sometimes around 10:00 p.m., sometimes later. I was away from home from 7:00 a.m. until whenever I got home routinely for more than a month. I was tired. Vince was worn out. But, we kept pressing on. And it was only because of His strength that we were able to press on.

Remember I shared Vince's response to these extra projects? I shared that he had told me that God had not brought me this far to leave me, and that he would do all he could to help. There was something always turning over in both our minds at the time—the vision that God had given Vince. Before he had met me, he knew me in a sense.

God had placed us in each other's life to help get each other to the next level. Vince had told me this from the very beginning. At the time in my brokenness I was thinking he could be my husband. He was different than any man I had met. I could tell that he felt the same although he expressed it as well. We connected on a spiritual level. We were both loving and caring and giving. We both loved God.

Yet, here was God loving both of us enough to refocus our attention whenever thoughts of being in a relationship came into play. It has not been easy, we certainly have had our confusing times, yet he and I were always reminded of what God spoke to him months before we came into each other's life—you'll be a blessing to one another. You will help each other get to the next level. Stay focused.

This brings me to this point. During this season in my life it was this focus that helped me make it through. I was definitely moving toward the next level. During this time in my "recovery" stage, God had been delivering me from relationship dependency and centering me upon the foundation of depending solely on Him. This brings me to the second point. Vince and I were purposed to be in each other's life. Sometimes we have sincere reasons or godly motives behind our thoughts, feelings, words, and actions—we must always be clear on whether or not this is intended.

My final point is this. God knew that Vince had gone through enough storms to help me navigate my way through the storms. He purposed a man to be a true friend to me. This is something I had never experienced. It was so hard at times for both of us. Yet, we kept our focus, and I was truly blessed me with a friend to help me get to the next level. Not only was he there mentally, spiritually, emotionally, financially, but even socially.

Now, finally around the middle of September two out of three of the projects were submitted. It was during this time that my purpose was revealed. Actually, I was engaged in a conversation with Vince after he had picked me up from work. He mentioned how much of a blessing all of the stress and strain of school, coupled with other issues really were to both of us. He mentioned how much I had grown since we had met and especially in this season. He shared his thoughts about several of the experiences in meeting women that were at crossroads in their lives. Yes, I met so many women, young and old, that were so comfortable in opening up to share their stories or challenges with me. Vince remembered this and had recognized early in our friendship his belief that I was definitely purposed for ministry on a large scale. My first message at the church I delivered had been on guess what? Virtue.

We talked about the amazing journey, and there was a peace in me that was so different. As we talked, I relived the process of discovery that God had used with each and every one of these women—through me—my own experiences. I recalled the dream I had shared with Vince and a few others where I was standing on a platform ministering to thousands. Not long after my dream, Shundala, my high school classmate, friend, and co-worker on the job, told me about her having the identical vision. Not to mention, the countless times my former pastor shared this with me. It was clear.

My purpose was clear. I was to minister to women everywhere who were broken, many not knowing that they are broken or how they got there. I was to serve God as a vessel to help these women move from being victims of brokenness to virtuous and whole in the Heavenly Father. This is when Vince said, "I told you that what we often go through is for other people. Everything that God does is to strengthen us but it's never about us, it's about God, and He is about delivering His people from bondage. Yo, you've made it through, and you will go higher. You need to write a book."

I did not see quite this clearly during the storm. I do know this: no trial or tribulation is greater than God's purpose for our life. Oftentimes it is because of our purpose that we go through the trials and tribulations. God allowed me to connect my passion for wanting to be a blessing to women and my desire to want to bless women's lives with the many storms I had faced in my life, starting from childhood. Upon deciding to write this book my passion to help women increased tremendously and instantly.

I submitted my last school project around the middle October. By the end of October, I had received the final grades for all the subjects. Guess what? I did not *just* pass—I passed them all! I will always remember how He placed a friend in my life that truly did stick closer than a brother—someone to help me weather the storms—someone fearless against the odds.

I was looking forward to December 14, 2006—my graduation day! When my name was called, I could hear my daughter screaming to the top of her lungs, "That's my mother!" I can never forget my son's big smile. I can remember the teary eyes of my friend, Vince. I will always remember his daughters' presence and laughter. And, oh, my friend Marisa—she made it possible for me to get to Montgomery, Alabama, that day. We all packed in her SUV and set out for Davis Theatre, where I walked across the stage to receive a reward for research, countless hours of studying, dedication, and perseverance. I give thanks to God, who is so awesome!

In all that happened during and before grad school, and no doubt after, God was preparing me for my special service to others. He was preparing me for ministry, in the true essence of the word ministry, which simply means "service." To live life based on serving others is a great place to be. It was Jesus who stated, "The greatest among you shall be your servant" (Matthew 23:11)

No matter what trial comes your way, continue to hold on to God's unchanging hand. There is no trial or tribulation greater than the power that God has bestowed upon you — you can make it through it, if you BELIEVE, PRAY, have FAITH, and take ACTION.

ONE
A ROADMAP TO VIRTUE...CRACKING THE SHELL TO BREAK THE YOLK

IF your parents were planning to take a family trip, where would you want to go? Some of you might say Disney World, White Waters, or Six Flags over Georgia, just to name a few. Your parents may use a roadmap to get to these places if they plan to drive their vehicle. Here is an illustration I would like to show you that requires a roadmap, which is used to help get people from one destination to the next. With this example, we will say that your parents decided to go to Disney World in Florida. Mind you, I am trying to go somewhere with this illustration.

Some of your parents will have shorter routes, and some will have longer routes. Since there are different routes, some of them may come to bumpy roads, dead end streets, have multiple hills to pull, and so on. But they will all get to their destination if the directions are followed as given on the roadmap. When they finally arrive at their destination, they will see how valuable the roadmap really is.

Some of them may turn around because the journey seems to long, and some may decide not to go at all. Now that is not to say that those who turn around and stop midways will not eventually get there. They might just need some encouragement along the way. Those who decide not to go will need an extra push.

The conclusion of this illustration is that God works just the same as a roadmap. He, in essence, is the roadmap. He wants to guide you girls from one destination to the next—take you from level to level—even higher than your mind can conceive. Many of you might get off course, lose focus, but you will all arrive there someday.

You see, you all started out when you were conceived in your mother's womb. What I mean by this is that when your mother was pregnant, it was you that was on the inside of her; meaning you was already a life that was waiting to be delivered into this world. You were all birthed with a purpose. You all have a destiny to fulfill. You will face difficult circumstances in life. More importantly, you were all born with the seed of virtue. You are all God's daughters, and He loves you so much, more than we will ever know.

There is something that I would like to share though—many of you are broken. To help you understand what I mean by broken, I will give you this analogy: If you were to pour water in a glass and it shatters as you pick it up off the table, then your water will spill, right? Once that glass shatters it can no longer be used for what it should be used for—and that is to drink liquid {water, juice, or soda} from. We as human are the same way—if we are shattered (broken), how can we be effective? I want you to understand that people can be broken in many areas of their lives. This would include mentally, emotionally, socially, or spiritually.

Here are some questions for you to consider:

- Are you broken?
- Would you say that your mother or father is mentally, emotionally, socially or spiritually broken?
- Are you striving to make sense out of the chaos in your life and move toward becoming whole?
- Have you been praying and hoping for change?
- Have you noticed any type of negative cycles that you have been repeating in your life?
- Are you having a hard time letting go of something bad {molestation, rape, criticized by your peers, etc.} that may have happened to you?
- Do you want God to heal you?

Out of the millions upon millions of girls in the world, there are a substantial number who are broken. The brokenness that you are experiencing could be as a result of something bad that may have happened to you. Whether it was your father, mother, brother, sister, extended relative, even a stranger who hurt or confused you—the adversity on your life has been crippling. You must become whole.

It is a blessing that you are now taking this very important step by picking up this book to overcome all the factors that have been hindering you. I want you to know that who you are according to God's will is more important and bigger than who caused your brokenness or in what ways you are broken, so go ahead, you can shout now. Your help is on the way. It is here, and it starts with you.

Teen girls, I was able to take a step toward deliverance and freedom, but this started with me admitting the problem and being open and honest about the details surrounding the problem. With this openness God blessed me to uncover many of the actions and the words that were at the root of my dilemma. Discovering the causes of brokenness is essential after you have confessed. Once you admit brokenness, God, along with your new understanding and knowledge in the matter—a desire for change with a commitment to change—will now move you forward to a new you.

When you are broken, it allows the devil to keep you in bondage. What I mean by bondage is that you are basically trapped into something. There is no outlet. You are held captive. Can you imagine that?

The devil will try to keep you in bondage by making you feel like you are worthless. He wants you to feel so shameful for what may have happened to you, whether you have been abused by a family member, a friend, or even if you have been talked about by your peers at school. I now realized that I was bound for so long, experiencing a life of unhappiness. I want to help you so that you want feel the unhappiness that I did.

You see, a girl who is broken on any level shows it on her face. When a person is broken it is also shown through their actions and conversation. How do you act? Do you act like a virtuous, godly teen girl? Do you cuss? Do you talk about people? Do you obey your parents?

I was once broken, and I did all manners of things that I was not proud of. Since I am now whole and free from brokenness, God has allowed me to see when something is wrong with another girl or woman. I can identify with the pain and hurt that you may feel. I was right where some of you are. But you can experience healing, too.

Someone helped me on my journey. I did not get to this place by myself. I thank God for blessing a ministering angel (my dear friend, Vince) to come into my life and help me understand that something was wrong with me—I was broken. Let me share with you that I did not fully understand the dynamics of my brokenness and how it played a major part in my doing things contrary to God's will, but I am grateful that it was revealed to me.

If you are wondering why you are broken, you may find that the root cause could be as a result of your mother, grandmother, and great-grandmother—they may have been broken. Have you notice that your mother did certain things (good or bad), and now you are doing the same things? Did your mother have a child as a teenager, and now you have one of your own as a teenager?

A lot of you may have witnessed some sort of abuse in the home when you were younger. Behind witnessing such horrible acts, some of you have been left scarred, and since you are at the brink of becoming a woman, I am convinced that you can experience healing and deliverance as an adult. You do not have to repeat the cycle of what your mother or grandmother or great grandmother did.

TRUE STORY

I know of a lady who had been abused from conception to adulthood. One day she felt the need to share her story. I can tell that she had been holding a lot on the inside that was ready to be openly expressed. I told her that she can find freedom, healing, and deliverance by admitting and confessing what has been causing her pain and hurt for more than 50 years.

She emphatically expressed how her father treated her so differently from her sisters. He was very mean, she said. He would buy her sisters clothes, shoes, and other things, without buying her anything. You know those kinds of things every child desires. Any tangible items she received came from her mother. "Why?" I asked. "I don't know why, but it was very hurtful to me," she said.

She went on to say that her mother had given her permission to go to a birthday party one night, and when she arrived home from the party her father had an extension cord ready to whip her. She ran up the street— over an older lady's house in the neighborhood—for safety. I asked, "Why did he want to whip you?" And she replied, "I don't know. My mother had given me permission to go to the party."

Later, at the age of 16, she graduated from high school. Strangely, when she arrived home on the night of her graduation, he viciously told her to leave his house. While she was excited and expecting to receive a reward for her accomplishment, like most high school graduates, he could only reward her with a gift of confusion and anger. This was a sad graduation gift, right? I was teary-eyed after hearing this.

After having to leave with nowhere to go, she was compelled to gain the help of this man who was a father figure in her life, yet he was a man whose eyes fell upon her at the age of fifteen. Oh, my God! She told him that her father put her out so she did not have anywhere to go. Yes, he offered her assistance by opening up his doors, but shacking up, or living with a man without being married to him, was not an option, she said. She told him she could not live with him unless he married her.

Now it was five months after graduation, she had turned 17 years old and was made his wife. I asked, "Why did you marry this man who was old enough to be your father?" and "Did you think about what you were doing?" "No," She replied. "I really didn't think about it until after I married him."

Later, she gave birth to her firstborn at the age of 18 — more children came later — more than she had planned to have. I asked, "Why did you have more than you desired?" and "Did you want to go to college?" Well, "He wanted more children," And, "Yes, I went to three different colleges, but I didn't finish."

Well, here is what was shocking—when she turned 30 years old; she learned that the man she thought was her father was not! Wow! This was interesting. One day, they had a heated argument and he yelled, "You're not my (blank) daughter anyway." He said it out of anger and bitterness, she said. This was the only man she had known from birth up to the point she was put out of his house—he was her daddy.

A few days later, an older lady down the street invited her into her home to show her a picture of her biological father. She was stunned, after seeing the picture of her stepfather and biological father taken together. They both went to the same church—and served as deacons. Sadly, she never had the opportunity to meet her biological father. By the time she learned of him, he had died. She was told that she had other sisters. As she reflected upon her childhood, she remembered the girls she went to the party with the night her mom gave her permission— those were her other sisters! She had seen them several times but never knew them beyond the neighborhood.

Now this lady's rights of knowing her father were taken away as a child. Her mother never told her because of the shame and guilt she faced as a result of going outside of her marriage to conceive a child—who was innocent all along—by someone who went to the same church their family were members of. After learning about her biological father, she asked her mother, but the truth was never offered. Her mother began to distance herself, only to hold the golden key to every child's right (isolation is not good when it comes to something of this magnitude; your child should know the truth). In her innocence, she was mentally, emotionally, socially, and physically abused by a man who never received her and a mother who held back the truth that was worth her knowing. Where do you think all this madness can lead to?

You see, she was conceived in adultery, never felt loved by her stepfather, never knew her biological father, never had a healthy childhood, forced to transition from a child to a wife within six months, and accept the abuse from a man who was more than twenty years senior to her. This was compounded abuse because it started with the man who raised her. This, in and of itself, is a lot to carry for year after year. She was broken, now fighting to find freedom.

In this instance, this lady was able to reflect upon her childhood to gain a clearer understanding of why she had been bound for so long. She was determined to uncover the seeds of brokenness and release the pains and hurts of her past, yet she did not admit (or truly not aware) that she was broken so that she could take the necessary steps toward freedom.

TWO
SHAME

SOME of you who are reading this book are living shameful lives. Many of you may have been victimized by some of life's challenges—you have been up and down emotionally. You have felt the shame of telling anyone about the things that you have encountered up to this point in your life. It is not uncommon to feel this way.

I can attest to feeling shameful. I was molested at an early age, not to mention the vast number of things that was shared at the beginning of this book. I felt that I could not tell anyone about what I was facing because no one would care or listen to me, and some would even talk about me.

As I grew older, I realized that I had to release the pain and hurt that I was carrying within my soul. I had to talk to someone. I knew there had to be someone in this world that I could confide in. I knew there had to be someone that would understand why I was executing the bad behavior in my early adulthood.

As I began to share my story, I learned that some people do care. Most importantly, God cares, even so that His Holy book tells us to "cast all your care upon him; for he careth for you" (Read 1 Peter 5:7). This scripture will give you confidence because He cares about what you have gone through and what you are currently facing; therefore, keep this scripture in your mind, heart and soul.

I want to encourage you to find someone you can talk to. Your mother can be the first person that you can share your pain and hurt with. If your mother is not around or you do not feel as though she will listen, then you can talk to an aunt, your teacher, your pastor's wife, your principal or some other positive figure.

You can find safety among a multitude of counselors. A counselor is not only limited to someone with a college degree that specializes in the area of counseling, it can be a special person that you look up to—someone that you know will give you good advice. You do not have to carry the shame of your past into your adult life. There is help, hope, and healing available to you.

THREE
GUILT

MANY of you are feeling guilty because you have taken full responsibility of someone else's actions. What I mean by this is that if you were innocently violated or suffered some other form of abuse (verbal, mental, emotional) or anything else that may have been unpleasant, you have literally blamed yourself for the bad behavior that someone executed.

Once you stop blaming yourself, you will feel much better. You will realize that what you encountered as an innocent child was not your fault. Therefore, it is perfectly fine to release the guilt. You do not have to hold it on the inside any longer.

You do not have to live this way, so "hold your head up." Do not beat yourself up anymore. Do not make excuses for someone else's actions anymore. Do not continue holding the guilt within. I want you to become free in your mind.

On your journey in life, you will come in contact with people who will blame you for everything. Usually when you cross the path of people like that, they are in need of a serious "makeover."

These kinds of people really need to search deep

within and totally accept full responsibility of their actions. But, even if these people choose not to accept full responsibility of their own actions, you don't have to become a part of their world by allowing them to make you feel guilty.

FOUR
HURT

HURT is another term that is often tied in with shame and guilt. As a motivational speaker, an author, and an emerging evangelist, I often share the dynamics of each of these terms when I am addressing girls and women.

There are so many of you teen girls who are wearing hurt "all over your face." Some people can easily detect that something is wrong with you when they look at you. Many of you show signs of discomfort, anger, and sadness…HURT.

Many of you are still hurting within because of something that happened in your past, and some of you are hurting because of what you are now facing in your life. You may have friends that "smile in your face," yet they talk about you behind your back, and some may even steal from you. You may have a boyfriend that always mistreats you. You may have an absent parent that keeps lying to you. You may live in a home with parents that fuss and fight all the time. There could be a number of things that's contributing to the hurt that you feel.

Are you ready to release the hurt that you are feeling?

I hope that your answer is "Yes." If so, I want you to know that you can release the hurt to your Heavenly Father.

Sometimes when you feel hurt, it does not immediately go away, but the more you talk to God, the less hurt you will feel. Remember, He will comfort you 24 hours a day.

FIVE
CRYING WHEN NO ONE IS AROUND

SOME of you teen girls may be overwhelmed with so many things. Sometimes you just want to get from around everyone and cry. You may have valid reasons to cry; however, some of you feel that crying is the ultimate solution to your problems. While crying offers a temporary relief, there is a great need to get to the root of your problem. What is causing you to be sad, discouraged, or troubled? I shared this several times in this book: you must talk to someone you can trust. You cannot close the door to those who can potentially help you.

I want you to understand that there are certain of life's circumstances and situations that can have the best of us (children and adults) feeling low. Most of our thinking will be consumed on whatever (lack of money, homelessness, a relationship breakup, sickness, parents divorcing, etc.) is causing sadness in our lives.

When you teen girls allow yourselves to stay in the "sad zone," you will not concentrate on the good things in life. You will not personally see yourself beyond your current situation. I have good news. The Bible says, "...weeping may endure for a night, but joy cometh in the morning" (Read Psalm 30:5). If you meditate on this scripture everyday (I literally mean every single day), you will learn that joy will transcend {rise above} everything that is causing you to "cry your eyes out."

SIX
VISUALIZING WHO YOU ARE

IT is important that you answer the following questions so that you can visualize (form a mental image of) who you are. The answers to these questions determine whether or not you see yourself in a negative or positive way.

- Can you see the true image of yourself?
- Do you see yourself in a negative image?
- Do you see yourself in a positive image?
- Do you see yourself as being an unattractive girl?
- Do you see yourself as being an attractive girl?
- Is it possible you may have low self-esteem? If so, where does that come from?
- Have you experienced something bad as a child?
- If you are in school, have your peers talked about you? Do they call you ugly? Do they call you fat? Do they call you nasty?
- Have you been told that you are not going to make it far in life?
- Have you been molested or raped?
- Did all this leave you broken?

I want you to understand that you are beautiful and smart—full of talent and gifts, no matter who says you are not. God saw fit to create you from the supernatural work of His spiritual hands. He shaped and formed you perfectly. In His creating you, He knew exactly what He was doing. That means you are definitely not a mistake. You possess so much, but because of the negative things people have told you, you have struggled with the acceptance of who you really are.

When a negative image of yourself have been planted in your mind, the tendency to attract negative things in your life will be great—the law of attraction is now in full effect. Your drive to move forward is not even there after the negative images have been planted. If you think about all the negative things that have been said or have happened to you up to this point in your life, I am certain it has hindered you in ways you could not believe.

For example, if someone told you that you are not beautiful enough to become a model, and you have been called ugly all your life, then this seed has been planted. You have now accepted that in your spirit because you do not feel that your nose is perfectly shaped, or your lips are not right, or you do not have the right texture of hair. Your hopes and dreams of becoming a model have now faded. Another example is if someone told you that you are not smart enough to obtain a diploma. You accept the fact that you have had certain learning issues, and now you do not feel that you are capable of learning college coursework, so you have a fear of going. Lastly, someone told you that you cannot sing. You begin to think about all of those times you could not stay in tune, so you have given up. Do you see how negative thoughts can produce negative images, which, in turn, lead to negative outcomes?

It is necessary to change the way you visualize yourself. If you will notice, actions are driven by visualization, and visualization is driven by thoughts. You see, to start you will **think** about the negative or positive, then you begin to **see** whatever that something is, then you paint a mental picture, if you will, and then you **act**. Did you get that? Here are the ingredients. **Think. Visualize. Act.** Whether it is negative or positive, that is totally up to you.

Just for a moment, I want you to think about all the negative things someone told you, whether it was your mother, father, sister, brother, friend, or anyone else for that matter. Now just as you painted a mental picture of all those negative things, and found yourself acting on it, I want you to replace all those negative things with positive thoughts. Do this in your mind now. You know what those things are, so go ahead, and picture them in a positive image. Can you see? What does it look like?

Is it the girl who has been called ugly who always dreamed of becoming a model, and now she is walking across the stage in a school pageant? Is it the girl who has had those learning challenges and now she's getting ready to obtain a diploma in her hand? Is it the girl who struggled with staying in tune in the choir and now she's getting ready to have a record deal?

I want to share with you teen girls that I was a woman who did not feel beautiful on the outside because my self-esteem had been attacked as a child. I was completely broken. I bore the hurt of what I was told as a child, and even what happened to me as a child. I carried that through my teens and into my early adulthood, but when I was made whole—totally delivered from people—I learned to accept everything about me. Outer beauty with respect to trying to please people can be an enemy of your destiny. It is never the outer appearance that matters; it is what is on the inside of you that will take you to greater heights and fulfill your ultimate destiny.

I want to let you teen girls know that once you are healed on the inside, the light of God will shine bright in your life and draw people to a wonderful, beautiful, anointed, spirit-filled teen girl. As you grow, you will realize that you are only a tool used by God, and you will begin to care less of what people think and say about you and more of who He has made and declared you to be. To add to this, you can start replacing all the negative images with positive ones. When you do that, you will see a major difference in your life.

FROM VICTIM TO VIRTUOUS FOR TEENGIRLS

SEVEN
YOU ARE PRETTY ENOUGH

WHEN you look in the mirror every morning you wake up, you should say, "I am pretty enough. I am a beautiful Gem and God loves me. He didn't make any mistakes on me." You have to come to a place in your life where you can honestly say that; knowing that you are pretty whether someone tells you or not or whether you get your nails done or not or whether you get your hair styled or not or whether you wear lip gloss or not.

Many of you are depending on someone to tell you that you are pretty; therefore, you find it hard to tell yourself. Some of you feel that you are not pretty enough unless you wear makeup. Some of you may feel that you are not pretty because you don't have the latest, brand-named shoes, clothes, etc. Remember, these are material things, and your beauty can never be defined by them.

Many of you have also grown to feel that you are not pretty because of how the media has basically defined beauty. Many of the music videos (and even some of the movies) of the day displays women wearing 6" stilettos, hair extensions, and basically their panties and bras. And because they say, "sex sells," many of these women have succumbed to this kind of lifestyle "for the love of money." They will wear less to bring attention to themselves.

Some of you who are caught up in the "music video" world think that you have to dress inappropriately, have certain facial features, and much more in order to be "pretty enough, "but I want you to know that you don't have to live in that kind of world — that world only gives you a false sense of who you are.

There is no need for any of you to compare yourself to anyone else, including those women in the music videos. When you do things like this you will try to mimic everything and everyone {some of the women who you may look up to as role models whether they are in person or on television} you see that is not a positive figure; therefore, it would not benefit you to try to become them. You are "pretty enough" just the way you are. You must carry this positive image of yourself in your mind daily.

If someone ever makes you feel that you are required to wear makeup and have all these material things to have the "pretty girl status," you need to know that this is untrue. You have to know in your heart, mind, spirit, and soul that you are "pretty enough" because God says you are. You were perfectly made in His image, and everything about our God is beautiful.

EIGHT
YOU ARE IMPORTANT

MANY of you feel that you are not important; that you don't mean anything to anyone; that your life does not matter. I have good news: you are important to your family, your true friends, and most importantly, you are a very special jewel to God.

Some of you may have experienced abandonment, lack of love, lack of support, etc. All these things can make you feel least important. You may have even had an encounter with someone who told you that you were not important. They may have told you that you are sorry, no good, stupid, and that you would never amount to anything.

I want to encourage you to be careful not to let what someone says to you discourage you because negative words can make you mad, sad or confused. You need to release it immediately and learn how to protect {to cover} your ears. You have to determine whether or not you are going to entertain {to hold in mind} what you hear.

You must practice ignoring anything that a person says to you that will make you feel like you are not important. You must also ignore words that are used to attack your character or your existence.

FROM VICTIM TO VIRTUOUS FOR TEENGIRLS

NINE
YOU CAN SHINE LIKE A DIAMOND

YOU are God's little daughter and you are just like a diamond. You may be thinking, "What is a diamond?" A diamond is "a precious stone consisting of a clear and typically colorless crystalline form of pure carbon, the hardest naturally occurring substance." It is a very valuable piece of stone. A diamond ring is even made with this piece of stone.

The reflection of a diamond ring can be seen from afar. It shines with a sparkling glow. That is amazing, isn't it? I want you to know that God will make sure you shine just like a diamond ring. This is to say, as a diamond can be seen among common rocks, you also will shine as a diamond among your family, community, at school—everywhere you go.

You are valuable just like a diamond, too. As you grow, I want you to always remember that. I don't want you to ever think that you are not valued. You are cherished, valued and loved by your family and so many other people. Most importantly, you mean the absolute world to God. He loves you more than you could ever imagine. He is the One who created you to shine like a diamond. I want you to say this, "I will shine like a diamond every day of my life."

TEN
YOU DON'T HAVE TO COMPROMISE YOUR VALUES

TO compromise simply means to "agree or settle." When you come to a place in your life that challenges you to shift to a settling mode (being in a comfort zone) because it feels right, usually there is more than what appears to be real on the surface. In some instances, those things that seem right are often fabricated because of selfish desires, and this can cause you to compromise with what has been presented to you.

Some of you may have found yourselves compromising your values for many different reasons. Your values may be integrity or dignity. Many of you have compromised your godly morals and values because of your lack of understanding. It is not uncommon for some of your values to be confused or distorted because of your upbringing, or negative experiences, which cause you to experience brokenness.

If you have been one of those teen girls who have been compromising your values; seeking happiness from others, you must stop it. God wants you to be happy on your journey, but happiness comes from within. The key to your ultimate happiness, peace and healthy self-esteem is finding and loving yourself, and becoming complete in

Him while you are a teen girl.

You do not have to feel like you are alone. It is in your mind. Your mind can take you anywhere you want to go, but teen girls, do not let the loneliness of mind take you in the bedroom to lie down with anyone other than your husband or to do anything else that can possibly ruin your reputation.

Now your thoughts of a husband should be further down the line. You have so much more to focus on right now. However, you can start striving to be your best so that when you grow into a woman and desire to be married, you will be ready. You are precious and valuable, and your body is the temple of God. You should not have to feel pressured by any male to open up yourself to fornication. Fornication can defile the body.

You should never think because you desire something so badly that you should accept anything that is presented to you. I do not care what it is—if it is not of God, it is no good for you. If you are one of those teen girls in the accepting mode, then you have clearly got it wrong. It is time to change gears, set standards, be patient and let God lead you on your daily path. Keep your mind focused on doing what is right. You could not even imagine what God has in store for you when you are doing what is right. He has many rewards for you.

ELEVEN
LEARNING HOW TO LOVE YOURSELF

WHEN you learn how to love yourself, you will accept every part of you. You will not feel unworthy, unappreciated, or misunderstood. You will have a great measure of self-respect, self-confidence, and a high self-esteem. You must understand though if you have low self-esteem, which is one of the most common barriers to loving yourself, it may be challenging; however, it can be corrected. Let me tell you how: you must tell yourself daily that you will love yourself no matter what.

There are many of you who may find that hard to do, but this is something that you must do. You have to speak to your heart, emotions, and mind—your entire being; knowing that you can love who you are and what you were created to do on your journey of life.

When you learn how to love yourself, you will not easily accept bad behavior nor execute bad behavior. You will know what it means to have morals. What I mean by this is that you will be concerned about your reputation, image, and character; ensuring that you are carrying yourself in a godly manner every day.

TWELVE
YOU CAN HAVE SELF-RESPECT

YOU should focus on respecting yourself everyday. You must understand that you cannot disrespect yourself and expect to be respected by other people. It does not happen this way.

There are way too many teen girls who are dressing in an inappropriate way, using bad language, and getting in all kinds of trouble. When anyone behaves in this manner, it shows the level respect that person has.

I want to give you two examples to help you understand the difference between a teen girl who respects herself verses a teen girl who disrespects herself. After I share these examples, I want you to determine which teen girl you think appears to have no self-respect.

Example 1: A teen girl gets out of the car to go into the grocery store. She is wearing a mini-skirt that is right below her bottom and a shirt that is revealing her stomach. As she approaches the store, she meets a group of boys who is coming out of the store and notices how she is dressed. One of the boys says something inappropriately to her, and then he asks for her phone number. She tells him to hold on, and she bends over and everyone can see her bottom, and then she walks over and gives him her number and whispers in his ear, "Call me anytime."

Example 2: A girl is walking down the hall at school, and she passes a group of boys who are contemplating skipping class. She is wearing a t-shirt and denim jeans that are loosely fit. One of the boys says something inappropriately to her, and then asks for her phone number. She politely says, "No thank you, I am not interested. She then proceeds to walk in her class.

Which one is an example of a girl who appears to have no self-respect? What do you think she can do to change her behavior? Do you think that she is seeking attention? Could it be possible that she has low self-esteem?

Many of you are seeking attention just like the girl that is described in example 1. And you may very well be seeking attention because your father may not be in the home or you may have a father present in the home, but he is abusive toward your mother (and his children), and a combination of other things. Some of you may be raised by a single mother who seemingly has no time for you. All of these things could possibly lead to "attention seeking" from other sources.

What I have learned over the years is that many girls (and women) desperately seek attention from those of the opposite sex. Sometimes when a person is seeking validation from someone else, they will do all manners of degrading things, and dressing inappropriately is just one of them. In order to combat (attack) this kind of behavior, it is very important that you love who you are so that you won't ever feel the need to be validated by anyone of the opposite sex. To be perfectly honest, you need to let God validate you.

FROM VICTIM TO VIRTUOUS FOR TEENGIRLS

THIRTEEN
YOU CAN HAVE SELF-CONTROL

YOU must learn to have self-control. To have self-control is one of the greatest preventions of yielding to the temptations, the sins of this world — gossiping, worrying, fornication, disobedience to your parents and other adults, etc. Do not let the temptations control your mind. You need to control the temptations in order for you to gain control over your thoughts. You must have a clear understanding of the liabilities of not being in control.

You need to cast down the imaginations and thoughts that come in your mind to tempt you to partake in actions contrary to living a productive life. It appears that whatever you think on for a period of time is what you normally act on.

Any thoughts that are contrary to pure thoughts can affect your mental, emotional, and spiritual health and well-being. Some of you may feel that thinking is of no harm; only acting upon the thoughts is harmful. Have you felt this way? You must not allow certain thoughts to set up camp in your mind. Whatever stays becomes familiar. Whatever becomes familiar becomes comfortable. Whatever becomes comfortable brings comfort in some way, even if it is the wrong way. By eliminating negative images you must destroy that image in your mind. No thought should grow in your mind to become greater than the thoughts that God knows what is best for you — even how you think!

Simply monitor your thoughts. Do not hesitate to attack any thought that is an attack on your peace, joy, strength, faith and obedience in the Lord. When a negative thought arises, replace it immediately with a positive one.

FOURTEEN
YOU CAN HAVE HEALTHY EMOTIONS

YOUR emotions can sometimes be good or bad, unhealthy or healthy. God has given some of you wisdom, which is basically using "common sense or good judgment," but you do not think rationally or objectively because of past and current pains/experiences, along with a number of other issues. Those dilemmas can cause you to remain stagnant, or not to grow, or to operate with the wisdom God has given you.

This can be reflected in some of your personalities, which is often influenced by your mentalities. I want you to understand that your personality is often shaped around your brokenness. It is this brokenness oftentimes, which creates a mindset, mentality that forces one in the opposite direction of truth, freedom, and peace.

Teen girls, some of you have made the same bad mistakes repeatedly as a result of your own thinking. Have you ever heard the saying, "A mind is a terrible thing to waste?" Well, many teen girls can find themselves caught in the negative emotions of the moment. These negative emotions are what drive your thoughts, and this thinking is what causes some of you to make bad decisions.

These poor decisions also reflect your lack of vigilance. What I mean by this is being watchful. You must observe what others say to you. More importantly, you must observe what you say to yourself in the silence of your thoughts. It is your thoughts that provoke the negative emotions you have as well as the negative thinking.

One of the symptoms of a bad mindset is how you negatively approach, respond, and behave in situations. This is possible because you will always move in a direction of what you think about most, regardless of whether that direction is negative or positive. But in this case, we are talking about wasting your thoughts, your time, and your energy in a way that is contrary producing a positive outcome. In essence, if you waste your time on negative issues, you are wasting your mind.

Now that you have identified the impact of a negative mindset, you know what is needed to challenge, correct, and move you toward a positive mindset. That movement should direct you toward success and freedom. When you think in the right direction, you can attract the right things in your life. Positive thoughts will attract positive results to result in your favor—in every area of your life.

I want to point out that so many of you have let your

negative emotions lead you into to harmful relationships. You do not have to experience the abuse from someone who does not respect you, who criticize you, cheat on you, does not love you, or outright mistreat you. When you open yourself up to this type of relationship, you may experience unhappiness, frustration, confusion, and manipulation. Once you form a relationship with this kind of person, later you may find yourself in a trap. Just like a spider's web (you know it is there), but when you try to eradicate (remove) it, you cannot always remove it because the web is now what I call a "web of emotions."

There are just as many teen girls who are faced with abusive relationships as there are women who face this issue. You must learn to grab a hold of your emotions, ensuring that you are feeding your mind with things that will contribute to healthy thinking. Just to reiterate what I shared earlier: You should not feel that you have to give attention to a relationship right now. You should think about what you want to be in life, how you plan to achieve your goals, what college you plan to attend, etc.

FROM VICTIM TO VIRTUOUS FOR TEENGIRLS

FIFTEEN
YOU CAN HAVE A HEALTHY SELF-ESTEEM

IT is so important that you teen girls have a healthy self-esteem. This will help build the confidence needed in order to accomplish great things in life. When you have a healthy self-esteem, it leads to positive, healthy thinking. Of course, you know, this is always good.

You will feel a sense of independence when you have a healthy self-esteem. You will never feel like you need someone to tell you that you are pretty, you are smart, you are important, you are talented, and so forth. Although these things are good to hear, it will not easily affect you if someone does not tell you.

However, if you are a teen girl who has low self-esteem, you probably see yourself as a "nobody," and you do not feel like you are worthy. You feel that your life does not even matter. Wait a minute—it does matter.

I want you to start learning how to appreciate who you are, value who you are, and love who you are. Going forward, you should start seeing yourself through the eyes of God. Once you do this, you will only see a beautiful person because that's how He sees you.

SIXTEEN
YOU CAN HAVE A POSITIVE ATTITUDE

It can be very challenging for you when you do not have a positive attitude. I am certain that you have heard that "attitude determines your altitude." When you have a positive attitude blessings and favor will manifest in your life. You will receive gifts, compliments, money, and a number of things, even when you are not expecting it—all because of your positive attitude. Can you remember those times your parents rewarded you when they told you to do something around the house and you did not have a frown on your face nor did you talk back? You may have wanted new clothes, shoes, money, or something else, and you received it all because of your positive attitude.

You must understand that people thrive off those who have a positive attitude. They like the positive energy that is released from that person being around them. Likewise, people will not want to be in your presence when your attitude is bad. It may be a challenge for you to receive help from people when your attitude is not pleasant, too. I am certain that you want good things to happen for you; therefore, you have to let God fill your heart with love so that the attitude problem that some of you may have can be erased.

If you are a teen girl who feels that you do not have a positive attitude because of something distasteful that you have gone through or now facing in your life, I want to encourage you to ask God to help you and not to let that "something" cause you to have a bad attitude. As a matter of fact, you can ask Him to fix your attitude. Trust me. He will do it for you.

SEVENTEEN
IT IS OKAY TO RELEASE THE ANGER

ITis never okay to be angry. Are you an angry teen girl? If so, think about what has caused you to be so angry. Do you believe that people want to be around you when you are angry? Do you like being around angry people?

When you hold anger on the inside of you, it can produce bitterness, hatred, and so many other negative things. When you are angry it can also hinder your personal and spiritual growth.

I want to let you teen girls know that it is okay to release the anger. You must first forgive anyone that has made you feel this way. When you do this, you can laugh more, love more, and pray more. You will soon find that your anger problem will subside.

In order to be a productive citizen, you don't want to continue being angry with people. You have to realize that some of the people who you may be angry with is actually happy with their lives. When a person is angry, they freely invite misery into their life. Is this you? If so, you can get free in your mind, spirit and soul. Release the anger so that you can move forward. There are great things ahead of you.

FROM VICTIM TO VIRTUOUS FOR TEENGIRLS

EIGHTEEN
DO NOT LOOK AT YOUR PAST

SOME of you may have found yourselves looking into your past too often. Yes, the past is part of your story, but it is not a part of the new story that God wants to prepare you for. He is concerned with your future. There are lessons that can be learned from your past to help prevent you from repeating the same cycles that you've repeated many times, but you must not allow the enemy, others, or yourself to take you back to relive the guilt, hurt, shame, or pain. It's the dawn of a new day for you, so I want to encourage you to embrace {cherish} it.

Looking back on your past can hinder you from receiving the many blessings. God wants to prosper you. He wants to turn your past hurts, pains, and disappointments into joy, peace, and happiness. He wants to use you so that you can bring Him honor and glory. He will erase your past, so turn it over to Him.

From this day forward, I want you to focus on your future. You can talk to God about everything and know that He will comfort your heart. Although you are young, you have so much to look forward to in this life. God wants to use your testimony so that you can help other girls. Your testimony could even give strength to adults, too. But if you hold on to your past, it will be much challenging to move forward and see what He has in store for you.

NINETEEN
IT IS OKAY TO FORGIVE

It is okay to forgive anyone who has wronged you. Whatever may have happened in your life to cause a seed of unforgiveness to be planted in your heart, you must not let it dominate your life. It is time to forgive. If you have not been able to forgive, then I am certain that you have found yourself wrestling with that something that deeply scarred you, even now. You have been reminded of that "something" that when spoken of; it leaves a bitter taste in your mouth.

Are you finding yourself getting upset about what someone has done to you or said to you? If so, you need to confront that issue head on and forgive whoever or whatever has caused you to be so bitter. Pray to God, and call out the person by name that may have violated or offended you. Ask God to forgive you and forgive them. You have to release it from your spirit.

Who has offended you? It's now not just the offense that haunts us, it's the fact that we allow the mental pictures of this offense to play out over and over in our heads. In essence, this is unforgiveness that repeatedly shows its' face. It makes you very angry when you think about it.

Forgiveness is not a matter of how you feel, it is a matter of God filling you with the power to release your hurt and release the person who hurt you. You cannot allow this issue to cripple you any longer. It is time to forgive. Do not go on year after year holding a grudge. It can affect your every thought. You may have heard the saying, "Let go and let God." (Read Matthew 18:21-22). What this is simply saying is "put it in God's hand." He knows how to work everything out in your life. He does not want you to continue having unforgiveness toward others.

TWENTY
YOU DO NOT HAVE TO FEAR

FEAR is a "strong emotion." There are so many people who have fear on a daily basis. The fear of loneliness, the fear of rejection, the fear of failure, the fear of the unknown are common "fear factors" that many people face. There are so many other things people often fear.

If you are a person who is fearful, I want to encourage you not to continue living in fear. Although some things may appear to be bad and make you feel as though you have to fear, you do not want your mind to concentrate on the negative things because "negative" can be manifested in your life.

I want to use an example to help you understand what I mean by this: Say you have to take a test at school in your least favorite subject, and you start to think and speak negative about this test, and you say, "I don't think I am not going to past this test because I am not a good in this subject." I want you to understand that your chances of failing this test will be great because you basically said that you would not pass it. What you must realize is that if you have fear of something, you will look for the worst to happen in your life.

I want you to understand the importance of having faith and not fear. What is faith, you might ask? It is "complete trust." You can start applying faith to every situation that you will encounter in life. God will teach you how to have faith (the opposite of fear) when you have a personal relationship with Him.

Faith can overpower anything that tries to make you fear. When you have faith you won't see things that appear to be bad in a negative light. Having faith with make you see the bigger picture. You will gain strength, and you will notice how less you fear. As time progresses you will have "no more fear." I must say that it will be a process, but God will always help you through any "process."

TWENTY ONE
YOU CAN OVERCOME ANY OBSTACLE

GOD has given you everything you need to overcome the trials and tribulations that come to harm you, but at the same time build you. The enemy (devil) will place obstacles in your path to make you give up. Some of you may have had to endure so much in your home, at school, and even when you go out in your community. You have been made to endure and overcome any obstacles in your path.

Let me give you an example to help you understand what I mean by an obstacle. Can you picture a mountain in your mind? What does it look like? Can you see over this mountain, or is it too high? Say for instance you have to climb this mountain to get to the other side. You have been told that something really extravagant is on the other side of it, and if you can get over there, you will be well pleased with the scenery. Besides, there will be great things when you get on the other side that you will see that will make you want to stay.

You really want to see it for yourself. Now since you have pictured this mountain, I am sure you are thinking in your mind, "How am I going to get to the other side of this mountain? It is too high?" Let me ask you a few questions "Are you ready to start climbing it? Are you fearful of the size?"

In this case, we will say this mountain represents all of the issues you currently face, which surrounds your brokenness. These issues make up this big mountain, the obstacles and stumbling blocks that stand in the way of your total freedom. Sometimes it is not easy to climb…sometimes it seems easier to just accept that you are not perfect. No human being is perfect, yet for wholeness you must be willing to be perfected. As this relates to that something in your way, you must develop a desire to overcome.

You may have a weakness right now that seems to have control over you. It is an obstacle in your life. You may not think that you can overcome it. You've come out for a season, but you have found yourself back in the same predicament all over again. Don't you know that God loves you, and He wants to make the very weakness you can't seem to shake your strength?

If you are in a certain environment or hanging around certain people that seem to pull you in the direction that captures that weakness, then you need a big shift in associates. Yes, that may include some of your friends that you hang around in school or in your community. You must see associates through God's eyes. You must ask: Does this person or group help or hinder my progress in gaining healing, deliverance, and wholeness? If your answer is "yes," then you need to start eliminating those people who don't have your best interest at heart.

TWENTY TWO
YOU CAN LEARN HOW TO PRAY

PRAYER is directly speaking with God. That means you can share any thoughts, pains, joys, and so forth, all by opening your mouth and speaking to our Heavenly Father. Prayer is important, necessary, and a powerful privilege, all conducive to a healthy relationship with God and personal growth. This is the greatest relationship you can ever have.

By communicating with God, your relationship with Him will grow, and it will allow you to be open in telling Him about your problems, asking Him for direction, and seeking Him whole-heartedly — through prayer. He has to be your first priority every day. When you pray continually throughout each day, it can increase the power within you. The power of prayer is truly an awesome thing. Having power allows you to defeat the enemy (devil) on every hand.

Just imagine talking to your earthly father about something that's been bothering you, whether it is about a friend, or even an experience that you had at school. If he loves you, he is going to offer support and comfort to help you get through it. Now how much more God loves you. How much more comforting can He be. He not only wants to help you get through your circumstances, but He wants to carry you through all of them. He is the comforter. So, are you broken? Are you hurting? Are you sad? Pray about it. Just like you can call your earthly father or other people to tell them about what you are going through, try calling God, no matter what time of day or night it is, He'll answer.

You cannot make it without prayer. It is important to you learn how to pray so that you can make it through some tough times in your life. I want you to know that you cannot always depend on someone else's prayers. There are times when you are going to have to pray to God for yourself.

When there is a lack of prayer during trying times, the burden(s) of circumstances are often compounded. What I mean by this is that one bad thing could be going on in your life, and before that ends something else could happen. You must remember that God did not say that you were not going to have trials, but faith and prayer can get you through them. Have you ever wondered why you can't seem to shake whatever it is that may have you bound? Have you ever experienced having a weak prayer life? If so—don't stop praying! You should not put any limits on your prayer life.

Teen girls, I want you to understand that God is so worthy of everything. All you have to do is have a sincere heart and a made up mind when you pray to Him about something. He's a phone call away. He will give ear to your cry. He's definitely worthy of serving. I mean, He's a God that will turn everything around in a matter of seconds, minutes, or hours. Remember, we can't put any limits on Him. He does whatever He pleases.

FROM VICTIM TO VIRTUOUS FOR TEENGIRLS

TWENTY THREE
YOU CAN EXPERIENCE WHOLENESS

YOU can experience wholeness as a teen girl. You do not have to carry this brokenness into your adulthood. Wholeness is available to all of God's children. When you become whole, it allows you to be all that God has purposed you to be. You can also help bring deliverance in the lives of others. Wholeness ultimately brings about freedom, which enables you to "think outside the box."What I mean by this is that you will begin to think for yourself and not let others control you with their thinking. You will realize the importance of only God controlling your life.

There is a certain level of peace that comes with wholeness. You know, when you are peaceful, it releases positive energy in the atmosphere—in the home, at church, at school—wherever you go. More importantly, wholeness will shed light on that seed of virtue (you) and make it flourish. I believe when you are whole, you can walk in your destiny, and there is a strong tendency to stay focused.

When any of us are broken the devil will use it to his advantage to keep us in a place of misery. The devil will tell you a lie; that God will not heal your broken heart, erase your pain, or dry your tears, but you have to tell Him boldly that "he is a liar." Having been a person who was once broken and now experiencing wholeness, I remember having that feeling that I would remain the same—that there was no freedom for me and I had to continue living in shame. I realized that I had to let go of the shame and guilt and see myself in light of who God created me to be—a virtuous woman who could live a free life and be an effective being. You will share the same experience if you desire wholeness.

7 DAY PRAYERS AND AFFIRMATIONS

DAY 1

Prayer: *Lord, I confess that I am broken, but I know that I am healed, delivered, and set free through your great healing powers. I decree that I am made whole. I thank you for giving me that faith to move beyond where I am in my life.*

Affirmation: *I will focus on moving in the direction of healing daily. I will see myself whole, happy, and confident.*

DAY 2

Prayer: *Lord, I thank you for giving me the wisdom and understanding of where my brokenness stemmed from. I thank you that I am no longer hidden in the shadow of brokenness. I thank you for giving me the power to break this cycle of brokenness.*

Affirmation: *I choose to live mentally, spiritually, and physically and not die mentally, spiritually, and physically.*

DAY 3

Prayer: *Lord, I thank you that my inner beauty reflects my outer beauty. Lord, I know that I don't need anyone to validate me – for I am a VIRTUOUS TEEN GIRL – filled with your spirit, but help me to accept and appreciate how you created me.*

Affirmation: *I am beautiful now, and forever will be. And I have a beautiful heart, and this I know. As a teen girl I can do anything I aspire to do because I am smart, intelligent, and gifted.*

DAY 4

Prayer: *Lord, I thank you for giving me your Word as a living principle for my life. I thank you that I can share your Word with my friends, families, and my enemies.*

Affirmation: *I will receive your Word daily in my heart so that I can apply it to my life and every situation that present itself to me.*

DAY 5

Prayer: *Lord, I thank you for blessing me to realize how valuable I am to you as a teen girl. Help me to stand on your Word and not compromise my values under any circumstance.*

Affirmation: *I will no longer compromise my values. I demand of myself respect, honor, integrity, and healthy thinking.*

DAY 6

Prayer: *Lord, I thank you for giving me wisdom. Lord, help me to use it every day.*

Affirmation: *I will continue to use wisdom throughout the rest of my life.*

DAY 7

Prayer: *Lord, help me to make good decisions daily. I thank you Lord for letting me learn from the bad decisions that I have made in the past.*

Affirmation: *I demand of myself a commitment to make good decisions daily. As I'm reminded of the bad decisions that I've made, and the consequences that followed, I will latch on to the positive energy and surround myself with positive people and make positive decisions.*

FROM VICTIM TO VIRTUOUS FOR TEENGIRLS

FROM VICTIM TO VIRTUOUS for TEENGIRLS JOURNAL

FROM VICTIM TO VIRTUOUS FOR TEENGIRLS

*

FROM VICTIM TO VIRTUOUS FOR TEENGIRLS

FROM VICTIM TO VIRTUOUS FOR TEENGIRLS

*

FROM VICTIM TO VIRTUOUS FOR TEENGIRLS

*

FROM VICTIM TO VIRTUOUS FOR TEENGIRLS

*

FROM VICTIM TO VIRTUOUS FOR TEENGIRLS

*

FROM VICTIM TO VIRTUOUS FOR TEENGIRLS

*

FROM VICTIM TO VIRTUOUS FOR TEENGIRLS

*

FROM VICTIM TO VIRTUOUS FOR TEENGIRLS

*

FROM VICTIM TO VIRTUOUS FOR TEENGIRLS

*

FROM VICTIM TO VIRTUOUS FOR TEENGIRLS

*

FROM VICTIM TO VIRTUOUS FOR TEENGIRLS

*

*

*

FROM VICTIM TO VIRTUOUS FOR TEENGIRLS

*

FROM VICTIM TO VIRTUOUS FOR TEENGIRLS

*

*

FROM VICTIM TO VIRTUOUS FOR TEENGIRLS

*

FROM VICTIM TO VIRTUOUS FOR TEENGIRLS

*

FROM VICTIM TO VIRTUOUS FOR TEENGIRLS

*

*

*

FROM VICTIM TO VIRTUOUS FOR TEENGIRLS

*

FROM VICTIM TO VIRTUOUS FOR TEENGIRLS

FROM VICTIM TO VIRTUOUS FOR TEENGIRLS

FROM VICTIM TO VIRTUOUS FOR TEENGIRLS

*

FROM VICTIM TO VIRTUOUS FOR TEENGIRLS

*

FROM VICTIM TO VIRTUOUS FOR TEENGIRLS

FROM VICTIM TO VIRTUOUS FOR TEENGIRLS

*

FROM VICTIM TO VIRTUOUS FOR TEENGIRLS

*

FROM VICTIM TO VIRTUOUS FOR TEENGIRLS

FROM VICTIM TO VIRTUOUS FOR TEENGIRLS

*

FROM VICTIM TO VIRTUOUS FOR TEENGIRLS

*

FROM VICTIM TO VIRTUOUS FOR TEENGIRLS

*

FROM VICTIM TO VIRTUOUS FOR TEENGIRLS

*

FROM VICTIM TO VIRTUOUS FOR TEENGIRLS

*

FROM VICTIM TO VIRTUOUS FOR TEENGIRLS

*

FROM VICTIM TO VIRTUOUS FOR TEENGIRLS

*

FROM VICTIM TO VIRTUOUS FOR TEENGIRLS

*

FROM VICTIM TO VIRTUOUS FOR TEENGIRLS

*

FROM VICTIM TO VIRTUOUS FOR TEENGIRLS

*

FROM VICTIM TO VIRTUOUS FOR TEENGIRLS

*

*

FROM VICTIM TO VIRTUOUS FOR TEENGIRLS

*

FROM VICTIM TO VIRTUOUS FOR TEENGIRLS

*

FROM VICTIM TO VIRTUOUS FOR TEENGIRLS

*

FROM VICTIM TO VIRTUOUS FOR TEENGIRLS

*

FROM VICTIM TO VIRTUOUS FOR TEENGIRLS

*

FROM VICTIM TO VIRTUOUS FOR TEENGIRLS

*

FROM VICTIM TO VIRTUOUS FOR TEENGIRLS

*

FROM VICTIM TO VIRTUOUS FOR TEENGIRLS

*

FROM VICTIM TO VIRTUOUS FOR TEENGIRLS

*

FROM VICTIM TO VIRTUOUS FOR TEENGIRLS

*

FROM VICTIM TO VIRTUOUS FOR TEENGIRLS

*

FROM VICTIM TO VIRTUOUS FOR TEENGIRLS

*

FROM VICTIM TO VIRTUOUS FOR TEENGIRLS

*

FROM VICTIM TO VIRTUOUS FOR TEENGIRLS

*

FROM VICTIM TO VIRTUOUS FOR TEENGIRLS

*

FROM VICTIM TO VIRTUOUS FOR TEENGIRLS

*

FROM VICTIM TO VIRTUOUS FOR TEENGIRLS

FROM VICTIM TO VIRTUOUS FOR TEENGIRLS

*

FROM VICTIM TO VIRTUOUS FOR TEENGIRLS

*

FROM VICTIM TO VIRTUOUS FOR TEENGIRLS

*

FROM VICTIM TO VIRTUOUS FOR TEENGIRLS

FROM VICTIM TO VIRTUOUS FOR TEENGIRLS

*

FROM VICTIM TO VIRTUOUS FOR TEENGIRLS

*

FROM VICTIM TO VIRTUOUS FOR TEENGIRLS

*

FROM VICTIM TO VIRTUOUS FOR TEENGIRLS

*

FROM VICTIM TO VIRTUOUS FOR TEENGIRLS

*

FROM VICTIM TO VIRTUOUS FOR TEENGIRLS

*

FROM VICTIM TO VIRTUOUS FOR TEENGIRLS

*

FROM VICTIM TO VIRTUOUS FOR TEENGIRLS

*

FROM VICTIM TO VIRTUOUS FOR TEENGIRLS

*

FROM VICTIM TO VIRTUOUS FOR TEENGIRLS

*

FROM VICTIM TO VIRTUOUS FOR TEENGIRLS

*